FROM PRISON TO PURPOSE

BY
JIMMY McGILL

Copyright © 2021 by Jimmy McGill. All rights reserved.

No part of this publication may be reproduced, distributed, or transmitted in any form by any means, or stored in a database or retrieval system, without the prior written permission of the author except as provided by USA copyright law.

Book design copyright © 2021 by Garrett Publishing a division of Garrett Media

Cover Garrett Publishing

Published in the United States of America

First published in 2019

ISBN 978-0-578-90871-7

Printed in the United States of America

To
Katie and Carter

It's only by God's mercy that I can give you the life I didn't have.

"For I know the plans I have for you," says the Lord. "They are plans for good and not for disaster, to give you a future and a hope."

Jeremiah 29:11

Special Thanks to Sharon Garrett

Without you, this book would have never been written.

Table of Contents

Chapter 1 1
Beginnings

Chapter 2 33
Prison

Chapter 3 51
Addiction

Chapter 4 65
Cracker Swagger

Chapter 5 81
Recovery

Chapter 6 99
Chelsea

Chapter 7 117
Cindy

Chapter 8 123
God

Chapter 9 129
J Dub

Chapter 10 137
Relationships

Chapter 11 143
Next Step

Chapter 12 163
The Recovery Clinic

Chapter 13 169
Full Circle

Chapter 1

Beginnings

Countless times I woke up in prison, sat up in my bunk with my head bent down, and wondered *how did I get here?* I suppose the answer lies in my past. I imagine you and I grew up in two very different worlds. Most people grew up in ordinary society. Not me. Some people say I came from a broken home, but to me it was just my home. I didn't know the difference. I will say it was an unhappy place. In fact, I never saw a happy home until the day that I broke into one.

As far back as I can remember, there were drugs in my life. Drugs and violence. My father loved me

Chapter 1

the best he knew how to love; however, his love for me was always secondary to his addiction. I seldom came first in his life. In making day-in, day-out decisions, my father didn't really factor in what was best for me; obtaining his drugs—when, where, and how—was the priority. If his decisions hurt me, then so be it.

The force that drove my father was his drug use. Before I understood addiction, I always thought he loved drugs more than anything. Now I understand the truth that he couldn't live without them. Once when I was released from prison, I told him that walking out of those gates was the best feeling in the world. He laughed, shook his head, and said, "No, Son, the best feeling in the world is a shot of good cocaine." This was the mentality in which I was raised. Did this make my dad a horrible man? Why was he consumed with drugs when other kids' dads were "normal"?

I come from a long line of addiction. My dad struggled with addiction because my grandfather struggled with addiction. My grandfather was a good man, but he was an alcoholic, totally consumed by the substance. I have heard that he was

Jimmy McGill

a bootlegger back in the day. I'm not sure about that, but I do remember that he loved his whiskey. He daily drank bottles of "Ancient Age." His addiction caused him to live in filth. I remember walking into his living room and the smell of urine hitting me right in the face. I have come to understand that my heritage was addiction, and this caused my childhood to be anything but normal. As a result, I have many, many painful memories.

Drugs and alcohol were as normal as food in my childhood. My first memory of drug use was my dad doing a shot of dope in my grandfather's kitchen. He was struggling to find a good vein, and so he told me to hold his arm off. For those of you who don't know, "holding the arm off" means taking both hands and wrapping them around the user's upper arm, squeezing as hard as you can so the vein will swell out for dope injection. I realize now that a father asking this of his son was very abnormal, but at the time it just seemed like normal life to the extent that I didn't even tell anyone about it. After all, don't all kids help their parents get high? Once my father was having trouble injecting himself, so he forced my cousin Kerri to take the sy-

Chapter 1

ringe and do it for him. He held a gun to her head as she inserted the needle, and she knew that if she missed his vein he would shoot her.

Unlike most people, Dad never seemed afraid of consequences. He literally did not fear anything or anyone, especially the police. Due to this fact, he was in and out of prison my entire childhood. The only way society could handle him was to lock him up. When he was in jail or prison, I would hang out in all the bars with "his people." I wasn't the kid that went to the playground or the park after school. My dad had introduced me to hole-in-the-wall beer joints where he did his thing. It was an environment of chaos, what most folks would have considered a place of misery. Not me. I loved it! I enjoyed being around the outlaw bikers, rednecks, gangsters, prostitutes, drug addicts, and thieves. In that atmosphere of child neglect, a thug was born. Everyone was hustling off each other, constantly trying to figure out who had what and how to get a piece of it. The deception thrilled me. Their war stories inspired me. I loved hearing about their fights, their shootouts with the police, their old prison stories.

Jimmy McGill

Everybody knew me because I was Thomas McGill's son. This brought a degree of prestige in the world I lived in, and I received a constant flow of attention. I was a prince among thieves, so to speak. I like to call this attention that I craved the first indication of my addiction. I craved it, I loved it, and I would do almost anything to get it. I wanted to fit in so badly with my older cousins Bubba, Jamie, Kerri, and Kelly that at an early age I tried to impress them by smoking the amount of weed they smoked and drinking the amount of liquor they drank. Once my cousin Mike (Kelly's husband) got me a bottle of MD 20/20, and I drank it all, just to impress him. I will never forget how sick this made me. His floor seemed to never stop coming up at me. I puked all over myself. Lying there, smelling my vomit, room spinning, feeling like I really screwed up this time, I asked God to make it stop. I remember thinking, *If I throw up one more time, maybe I will feel better*. I made empty promises to God and just hoped that he would accept all my bargaining. This is just one of many examples I could tell you about how I went to drastic lengths for affirmation. Receiving attention

Chapter 1

changed the way I felt about me; and, well, I just didn't like me.

Not only were drugs and alcohol a common part of my childhood, violence was the norm in my environment. My father was a violent man. Everyone feared him, including me. It seemed like all the tough guys needed his help or owed him a favor. My first act of violence happened when I was four years old. We lived in a trailer park in the East End part of Little Rock, and I stabbed the kid next door in the shoulder with a potato peeler. He was a few years older than me. I brought a butter knife and a potato peeler outside so we could cut twigs off of a small tree branch. He put the butter knife in his back pocket. After a few minutes, I decided I needed the butter knife instead of the potato peeler. Instead of just telling him I wanted to see the butter knife, I grabbed it because it was sticking out of his back pocket. When I did, he slapped my hand, and in my book, that was a huge mistake. The way I saw it, that was my knife that I brought out of my house, and so I raised the potato peeler and slammed it down into his shoulder. I will never forget the "butt whipping" my dad put on me for

Jimmy McGill

that stunt. Looking back, I think he was probably mad because the police got called, not because I stabbed the kid. After all, violence was his way of communication. Countless times he would get paranoid and make everyone in the house be quiet, basically holding them hostage and accusing them of communicating secretly. He would keep them until they admitted it, whether they were guilty of it or not. Violence was a major force that formed the way I thought about life and relationships.

My birth mother Cindy was pretty much tortured by my dad. He shot her toe off and beat her with a hammer, and finally when I was six months old she left. I'm sure leaving her baby was one of the hardest things that she ever did, but she knew if she took me with her, she would never get away. Dad then gave me to Linda, who became my adopted mother. Linda was a good woman. She did not drink or do drugs. You're probably wondering how someone like Linda ended up with someone as psycho as my dad. Simple. He held her hostage. She was a carhop at a fast food joint. When she brought him his food, he literally took her, and *that's all she wrote*.

Chapter 1

I was around eight years old when we had to go on the run. Linda, Dad, my Uncle Roy (Dad's brother), and I took off to Georgia. We lived in a place called Ellabell. I remember that one night I was in the living room, and my dad came in and asked where my mom went. I didn't know she had gone anywhere. Apparently she and Dad had gotten into a fight, and Dad had decided to kill her. She had run out the door and into the woods in fear for her life. She ran through the woods barefoot, blinded by darkness with thorns tearing her face, arms, and feet. The next morning Dad didn't wake me up for school, and suddenly I heard over a loudspeaker, "Thomas McGill, come out with your hands up!" The scene unfolded as if I were watching a movie. Uncle Roy raced like a cheetah to an unsafe hiding place under the bed. The police came in and took my dad and my uncle that day.

Dad was gone, and I wasn't bothered too much by that fact. Mom and I moved to Port Wentworth, Georgia. My life, however, didn't really get much better. My dad's sister, my aunt Louise, lived in Georgia, and she and mom worked together at

Jimmy McGill

Gulfstream Aerospace. They decided to go out for dinner one night and left me with a babysitter. The babysitter, who was supposed to be watching me, was next door hanging out with some guy. A kid named Trey was spending the night with me. Trey was on my Nintendo, and I was outside shooting a 22 rifle that my father left me. I went in the house, swung the gun around, yelled, *"Trey, check it out,"* and suddenly the gun fired. It was unintentional, yet I had shot someone. In the mercy of God, the bullet missed his heart by two inches. He stood up in my living room, screaming, blood gushing out of his shoulder, and tried to get through the door. All that was on my kid's mind was not getting into trouble. I freaked out! I tried to cover his mouth and get him to quiet down and stop screaming. I kept telling him that it was an accident and things would be okay. That didn't really work, and mom arrived as the ambulance was leaving with Trey. I remember being terrified that my life was over. Surely I was going to get a spanking to last a lifetime or grounded for the rest of my life. I was simply scared. I wanted to be near my mom, but I feared her reaction. After all, this was pretty seri-

Chapter 1

ous.

I didn't get in any trouble for shooting that kid. Poor Mom just flat out didn't know what to do with me.

We jumped from Port Wentworth to Garden City, Georgia. I hated Garden City. We lived in an apartment complex called Plantation Townhouses. It was full of kids, and I did not fit in. I moved in there acting tough and pretending to be as cool as I thought they wanted me to be. That simply led to me getting beat up and bullied a lot. There was one particular kid named Josh. He was tall, and he wasn't afraid to fight. I was on the receiving end of his aggression many times. The girls in those apartments didn't seem to like me either, probably because all the boys would jump me. I remember walking home from school one day with my Sony walkman on, listening to a music tape, and out of nowhere a whole group of kids ran up on me. They had literally been looking for me in the apartment complex. Josh grabbed me from behind, and he picked me up off of my feet and held me helplessly while this girl was slapping me in the face. I imagine those experiences shaped the person I was slowly becoming. Those experiences are the reason I made my mind up to never be a victim of someone else's aggression again.

Life just sort of kept pushing on without a lot of change—different place, same story. There were some housing projects called Westgate behind our apartments. Westgate was full of kids in my school who were selling dope and gang banging. There was something attractive about that, something familiar. So I would talk to them and hang out with them a little bit. I was always desperate for attention from the "cooler" kids. One day on the steps of my school, one of the kids from Westgate took his baseball cap off, and the inside of that cap had small bags of crack rocks stapled to the inner lining. I thought that was so cool, and it wasn't long before I was putting some of my mom's medicine into small corners of a Ziploc bag. I was trying to fit into the image of a dope boy. I had no clue what the medicine was, didn't care. It probably wouldn't even have gotten anyone high; shoot, it could've been blood pressure meds for all I knew. I had no idea what I was going to do with the bagged-up, fake dope. I just carried it around with me, waiting

Chapter 1

to get into trouble with it.

It was a different school with new kids. I had zero people skills and absolutely no idea of how to treat people or talk to them, let alone how to make friends. I pretended to be cooler than I really was and tried to fit in, but regardless of how hard I tried, I failed. Unlike my old man who couldn't care less what others thought of him, I wanted to be with the cool kids. I couldn't understand the reason for it, but I daily got beat up and bullied by the other kids. This was an incredibly sad season of my life.

A little later during this general time frame, I experienced childhood sexual abuse from a male babysitter. My molester did not have horns and a devil's tail. He was not scary. I wasn't forced by my abuser, but I was groomed—looking back I can see he coerced me into allowing the behavior. This was yet another situation in which my need for attention was used against me. This man showed me attention and was kind to me. I was so bruised and wounded from the constant bullying by the kids at school. He was around sixteen, and as a nine-year-old kid who didn't fit in, I was vulnerable to his ad-

Jimmy McGill

vances. I was so desperate for someone's approval that when he suggested I touch him, I did. I didn't know any better. Those experiences would go on to haunt me, and in reality, fueled the drug use in which I was soon to drown.

By the time I was ten years old, I was huffing gas and smoking pot. I had such an internal conflict going on inside of me. On the one side I pretended to be hard and cool, while on the other side I battled shameful thoughts of what my father would think of me if he knew about the babysitter and the sexual things that I had let happen to me.

Not long after all this, my first serious interaction with the law occurred. In a sporadic and lame attempt to be one of the cool kids, I took pills out of my mother's medicine cabinet, crushed them up, and put the powder in a bag. I sealed the bag with a lighter and an old music cassette tape case like my father used to do when he was bagging up dope. Bam! I had something other kids had now. So, I snuck out that night and decided to hang out by the gas station in front of the apartments in which we were living. About 10:00 p.m., a Garden City police officer rolled right up. Can you imagine

Chapter 1

the thought that must have run through his head? Here I was, standing in an empty parking lot of a closed-down gas station way past my curfew, trying to look cool. To top it all off, I had put on some of my mom's gold jewelry so I would really look cool.

Next thing you know, the police were searching me and I was arrested for possession. I was thrown into a juvenile detention facility in Savannah, Georgia. I was only 10 years old at the time, and let me tell you, I was screaming inside. Tears were rolling down my face for days. I was locked in a box, alone and scared. I remember begging God to return me to my momma. For the first time in my life, I was completely alone both mentally and physically. I was trapped in a place that I knew nothing about and with absolutely no one to give a damn about how I felt or what happened to me. The more I cried, the more the other kids laughed. I was a helpless, young boy who wanted his mom. After about a week of intense experiences, I was finally released to my mother. The relief was incredible; but even after all of the prayers, pain, and tears, I promptly forgot all about the entire experience. I forgot every bit of desperation that I had

Jimmy McGill

temporarily felt and went right back to behaving as if nothing had ever happened.

By the time I was 12 years old, I had stolen all my mom's jewelry. An older guy pawned it for me, and I used the money to shoot pool and play video games at the local arcade. I would frequently steal money from Mom's purse. Grabbing a twenty-dollar bill was commonplace. Today I understand that I was simply modeling the behavior of my father. I followed in my dad's footsteps, taking what I wanted regardless of who it hurt, without even a twinge of conscience. I held his mentality that the strong had no need to ask permission; that only the weak had to ask for what they might need or want. After all, I was trying to convince myself that I was not weak. When I was about thirteen, my mom sent me back to Arkansas. My dad had gotten out of prison, and I went to live with him. In her way of thinking, I had put her through enough hell, and in truth I had. She would tell me no when I wanted something, and I would throw a fit, scream, argue, beg, whatever I had to do. She would give in because I just wouldn't stop. She tried everything with me. She did the best she could with me, but I

Chapter 1

made it impossible. She tried to put me in a children's home for a little while. She tried spanking me or grounding me, but nothing worked. I was the wrath of hell packaged in a child's body. Separating from me was her only option as far as I am concerned.

It would be seventeen years before Linda and I spoke again. Back then I didn't care. To this day, looking back on those memories still tears up my heart. I often wonder: if I had had a different male role model in my life during that time, would my life had been different? For a long time, I considered my environment and my culture to be the reason my life was a mess. Today I know I'm a product of my decisions, not my environment. I'm sure I could have been given a better chance at making good decisions had I grown up with more positive influences; however, my choices are my responsibility.

By the time I was thirteen years old, I had witnessed more violence than most adults do in a lifetime. I had experienced more sadness than any other child I knew. The crazy part about all this is that I had no idea that my childhood was abnor-

Jimmy McGill

mal. I was oblivious to the fact that my life was full of pain and sorrow. I was so used to the loneliness and hurt that I was immune to it. You only know what you know, and you can't miss what you never had. I was content with a life that most kids wouldn't be able to survive.

My cousins Kelly and Kerri would try to take care of me the best they could, when they could. I would go stay with them for days at a time. They were cool and I was safe with them. They always had pot. One time I was playing poker at age thirteen with my cousins, and I had smoked so much pot that I couldn't move from Kelly's couch. I was stuck, literally. The adults were smoking, playing cards, and laughing at me.

Looking back, there is absolutely no reason in the world for any adult person to ever be as drunk as I was at thirteen. I remember lying as still as a dead person in my own vomit, more times than I can count. I remember the aftertaste of food and liquor in my mouth, spittle dripping off my face, and the room spinning. I would pray to God to make it stop and promise Him over and over that if He would, then I would never again get drunk.

Chapter 1

And I would live up to my word all the way to the next weekend. It was easy to drink cheap wine like Mad Dog 20/20 or any liquor, really, if it had a sweet taste instead of a burn. I would go and get bags of pot from my father's friends, and at one point in my seventh-grade year my Dad gave me a half pound of marijuana. I felt like I was the kingpin. I literally lived out fantasies in my head. You couldn't tell me anything at that time; I was all about that life.

I got my dad to give me a set of handheld hanging scales and a box of Ziplock sandwich bags and got after it. I knew each quarter should weigh eight grams. The first sign that I was a horrible drug dealer was when I gave it away just to fit in and make people like me. The second sign was the fact that I smoked what I didn't give away; and I was still broke after the pot was gone. Some kingpin, right? Over time I never got any better at being a dealer. By the end of this book, you will more than likely agree that I was probably the least profitable and dumbest criminal to ever exist.

Now every crime I committed was in pursuit of a drug. My solution for changing the way I felt was

Jimmy McGill

drugs. Unfortunately, drugs did not change the circumstances surrounding my life. I consider a drug to be anything that changes the way I feel: any mood- or mind-altering chemical or anything that interferes with me being a productive, responsible person—whether or not it is a narcotic. As I have alluded to earlier, the first drug I ever used was not a chemical; it was attention. I always wanted to feel needed, wanted, and valued. The man who was supposed to give me these things was too busy showing it to his own addiction. I grew up with a huge hole inside of me. I slowly began to fill it with anything I could. I had always searched for validation; it was a Band-Aid for my depression and loneliness.

I missed a lot of school. I hated school, and when I did go, I showed up and showed out. I didn't have very many consequences at home for getting into trouble at school. I did what I wanted to do whenever I wanted to do it. I got jumped a few times in the seventh and eighth grades, always by the older kids. My ability to fight and my mouth didn't match up at the time. There were times that I was beat up by kids because I brought my mouth

Chapter 1

and attitude to school where my father's reputation was nonexistent. Suddenly I had to defend myself with no giant shadow behind me to offer protection. However, there were also times that I was bullying weaker kids. As I got older, the bullying slowed down for the most part. I learned along the way that I had to have the right friends. Now, try to understand that what most of you would consider the "right" friends are not the kind of "right" I'm talking about. I hung out with the kids who weren't afraid to fight, who didn't care about anything, and who were notorious for breaking the rules. To me it seemed like all the bullies feared the kids who did drugs. So, that is who I hung with. We would skip school, smoke pot by the dumpster, and smoke cigarettes on campus. We would get caught, get suspended, then do it all again. For a while, my older cousin Jamie went to the same school that I attended, and he was extremely popular. So, even though I was only in the seventh grade, all the ninth graders knew who I was. At that time, all of the girls were in love with my cousin Jamie, and most of the boys were in love with my cousins Kerri and Kelly. Like any good manipulator, I tried

Jimmy McGill

to use that to my benefit, although I didn't have much luck.

Finally I just wouldn't go to school. All I did was skip classes and have fun. I didn't like anyone who tried to tell me what to do. I hated getting up and knowing I had to be on time. When I got to school, I would walk in the front door and right out the back. Then I would walk all the way through the woods back to my grandfather's house or to my aunt Juanita's house, about a five-mile hike. I started skipping school with the wrong kids, and that's when the real trouble started. One particular kid named James was down for some things that I had not yet been exposed to—like breaking into houses and stealing stuff. Then the occasional break-in transitioned into daily criminal activities. We were robbing houses, stealing guns and anything we could loot for extra money.

James was later convicted on a murder charge when he, his girlfriend, and his mother beat someone to death. I learned some pretty bad habits from him. During my first trip to Varner Prison Unit in Grady, Arkansas, I reconnected with him. James eventually made parole on the murder rap,

Chapter 1

only to continue living the thug life. It was the only life he knew. Now, decades later, I believe he's somewhere doing a massive amount of federal time.

To give you an idea of my track record during this season of my life, on the following pages is my eighth-grade disciplinary file.

At fourteen I began breaking into the houses in my community on a daily basis. My lack of regard for people caused me to destroy their homes. I had no idea the devastation that I was causing these hard-working people. Currently I spend my life trying to redeem and amend my past. I was two years into my recovery when my first honest apartment would get burglarized and I would experience a small taste of my reckless behavior. I had no real need for money at that time in my life; I had no major drug problems. The only possible reason for my behavior was an overwhelming need for validation. By this time, people pleasing was second nature to me. I was so desperate for approval that I was willing to put my life in jeopardy. I cared more about others' opinions of me than I did my own life. This mentality led me to eventually land

Jimmy McGill

DISCIPLINE RECORD OF JIMMY McGill

Date	Teacher	Incident	Action
9/22/88	Langford	Was placed in D-Hall for misbehaving for a substitute and did not show	Conference & placed in D-Hall
10/4/88	McGaha	Misconduct while D-Hall students were in the cafeteria	1 day to D-Hall
10/28/88	Langford	Dispute with another student that caused a loud disturbance	2 days to D-Hall; next time temporary suspension
10/28/88	Lee	truancy - skipping 8th period-off campus in trailer park	Parent/Administrator conference
11/7/88	Lee	Took some passes of Mrs. Ford's desk. The sub caught him with them. He had them in his pocket	Temporary suspension and parent conference
11/10/88	Revis	Jimmy was talking without permission; sent him out to the hall; he tapped his pencil disrupting the class; distracting the class inside the room. Told him to quit; he kept on. I went outside in the hall and told him if he kept it up I would send him to the office. As I walked back into the room, I heard one last "crack". I went back out into the hall. He had broken his pencil in half.	3 day suspension
11/10/88	Lipsmeyer	3rd unexcused tardy	Conference & warning
12/5/88	Lee	Playing around	1 day to D-Hall
12/12/88	Lee	disruptive behavior in class	2 days to D-Hall
12/16/88	Powell	smoking on campus	5 day suspension
1/11/89	Hardman	hit another student as they left class. Was warned that if this behavior occurs again he will lose the privilege of walking to his classes unescorted.	
1/13/89	Dobroth	3rd tardy to Ms. Dobroth's class.	Conference & warning
1/18/89	Dobroth	Not having supplies	1 day to D-Hall
1/18/89	Phelps	Making fun of a 9th grader in D-Hall	suspended for 3 days
	Dobroth	Lack of class materials	
	Hardman	Annoying to classmates; excessive talking, mischief	
	Lipsmeyer	Talking and shooting paper wads in A-Hall	
1/27/89	McGaha	Talking and misconduct in D-Hall	Corporal punishment
1/26/89	Stephens	Told the teacher that the school and class "sucks" Annoying to classmates, lack of materials, lack of cooperation, rude, discourteous, restless, inattentive, excessive talking, mischief	Conference with guardian. Working with her on medication. Misconduct cannot be permitted.
2/8/89	Drury	3rd tardy to Mrs. Drury's class	Conference & warning
1/26/89	Stephens	Shooting rubber bands in class	2 days to D-Hall
1/31/89	Drury	excessive talking	1 day to D-Hall
2/2/89	Hardman	Spitting	1 day to D-Hall
2/14/89	Neel	Talking loud in class	1 day to D-Hall
2/14/89	Hardman	Threatening another student, excessive talking	1 day to D-Hall
2/22/89	Hardman	Not following directions; being disrespectful to teacher	1 day to D-Hall
2/23/89	Hardman	Not following directions; being disruptive to others	1 day to D-Hall
3/1/89	Stephens	Excessive arguing in class	3 days to D-Hall
3/1/89	Riggs	Talking	1 day to D-Hall
3/10/89	Hanson	Not following directions	1 day to D-Hall
3/15/89	Riggs & McGaha	Jimmy was responding to my questions in a rude, discourteous way	Conference with Jimmy

23

Chapter 1

3/17/89	Stephens	Talking in class (excessive)	1 day to D-Hall
3/21/89	Stephens	Called another student a "Bitch"	Morning D-Hall
3/24/89	Drury	Fighting in hallway	Assigned D-Hall
4/13/89	Stephens	Did not show for D-Hall	Will be in D-Hall on 4/13/
4/17/89	Drury	3rd tardy to Mrs. Drury's class	Conference & warning
4/18/89	Riggs	3rd tardy to Ms. Riggs' class	Conference & warning
4/18/89	Hardman	Insubordination	Stern warning
4/19/89	Calhoun	Excessive tardiness	1 day to D-Hall
4/26/89	Revis	Did not show for D-Hall 25th or 26th time	he was absent
4/27/89	Riggs	Jimmy is acting in a rude manner. When he was told to stop talking, he began making faces which I noticed and will not tolerate. He has been warned twice today	Conference & warning
4/27/89	Hardman	Theft - candy bar taken from another student and seen by a student.	3 day suspension
4/28/89	Hardman	Eating candy in class; refusing to give candy up when asked	Combined with other report
5/10/89	Riggs	excessive tardies	No action

Jimmy McGill's disciplinary file

in the penitentiary. I skipped school with the wrong crowd one day, went into the wrong house, and I was arrested. I was charged with burglary as a juvenile.

I confessed to that burglary and a couple more even though I really wasn't guilty of all they charged me with; but at the age of fourteen after being coerced and abused by law enforcement, I really didn't know what else to do. At first I was not going to admit to anything, but they convinced me otherwise. Looking back, I now understand that they had no evidence to convict me. However, the detective facilitating my interrogation inside the interview room at the Pulaski County Sheriff's Of-

Jimmy McGill

fice wasn't going to let it go down that way. He got tired of hearing me say, "I don't know," and as I sat handcuffed in the closet-sized interview room, this grown man with a badge stood over me, grabbed me by my neck, and choked me against the wall, yelling in my face how he was going to "eff me up" if I didn't start talking. I couldn't believe what was happening, and I felt completely powerless and helpless. I felt I had no choice. I told him everything he wanted me to tell him. I even confessed to things that I never did. I know today that my criminal history was born out of my own actions, but the actions used to build the case against me were completely illegal.

After my arrest I was thrown into juvenile detention. I only stayed there for a couple of weeks, but there I was exposed to something new—neighborhood gangs. From the start gangs intrigued me. The members all seemed to belong to each other, and no gang member ever seemed alone. This was what I craved. At the time I was facing serious felony charges, and the other kids told me that I was going to go to training school, which is basically kid prison. That scared the the day-lights out of me.

Chapter 1

One of the kids said, "Tell the judge you smoke crack; they will let you out and send you to rehab." I had never seen crack in my life, but by the time I walked in that courtroom I was an expert on how to get it and how to smoke it. I was a good liar. Sure enough, the judge sent me to rehab—thirty days and then freedom. Seemed to work out for me.

There was only one problem. My dad was back in prison, so I had nowhere to go. However, my dad's sister, Aunt Juanita, came to my rescue, or so I thought. I'll tell you more about my aunt Juanita later. She was an incredibly positive influence in my life. For now, back to the story. She didn't let me stay with her but decided for me to go to the Arkansas Baptist Boys Ranch in Harrison, Arkansas. Now for a city boy that was "hood," that seemed like a living hell. There were eight kids living at the ranch at that time, and in reality it wasn't that bad; we had lots of land and horses. They would let us go to town and to the mall. They were good to us, but I was a troublemaker and as always bucked the system. One day I thought I was John Wayne and devised me a getaway plan. I was going

Jimmy McGill

to steal a horse and ride back to North Little Rock. My favorite horse was an old Appaloosa show horse named Smokey. Smokey and I were about to ride out from Harrison, Arkansas. Now, from Harrison to North Little Rock is about a three-hour drive by automobile. The plan was working great until the horse would not walk over the guard rails in the road. Let me just say that it didn't end well. I told you earlier that I was not a smart criminal.

When my attempted escape did not work out, I resorted to what I always did, rebel. Six months later they had had all of Jimmy they could stand, and they dropped me back off at the juvenile detention center in Little Rock. A few hours later, I was in the Pine Bluff training school. It really was hell on earth. They called it little Saigon. For those of you who don't know about Saigon, let me tell you, it was a battlefield. Twenty-four hours a day, seven days a week the kids were at war with each other. We would not just fight each other; we would jump the staff as well. The chaos made it fun. Little Saigon was a perfect name for that environment! It was pure chaos. It didn't matter who you were or where you were from, everybody was going to get

Chapter 1

their turn at getting beat up. It was only a matter of time. You were going to get jumped. It basically just depended on whose day it was for action. It was a dog-eat-dog mentality. The strong preyed upon the weak, and you were only strong if you ran in a pack—so that's what I did. Hands down, it was the worst place I've ever been. Little did I know that the Pine Bluff training school would be worse than any prison time I would ever do. I ended up going to prison multiple times. You could put each prison trip in a pot, and it still wouldn't equal a tenth of what I went through in training school.

I was there for almost two years. During my luxurious stay at the Arkansas Division of Youth Services, I became a gang member and I loved it. For the first time in my life, I felt like I belonged to something. Thinking through my past, I can trace my life of incarceration all the way back to trying to fill a void of validation, desperately trying to feel wanted and important to those around me. Being a gang member gave me those things. We were a likeminded community, a group of kids just like me, lonely and desperate. We all came from

Jimmy McGill

nothing, but put us all together and we were something. We were family. I wasn't alone anymore. Because I was a white boy, I had twice as much to prove as others. I was banging in a world that was completely foreign to me. So, I went twice as hard as anyone else, and I jumped stupid twice as fast (meaning I was quicker than anyone else to show my butt, mostly for the sake of whoever was watching). I was always the first kid in the bunch to talk trash and the first to swing. I was too stupid to realize where this was going to lead me. If only I had been able to tell the future, I would have known that this was only going to lead me into total turmoil and chaos.

At 16 I was released. This time, getting out was totally different because I brought that gang mentality back to North Little Rock. Although I was really just a nerdy, scared kid trying to fit in, I was hardened. I had changed on the inside. My image had changed, my mentality had changed, and my name had changed. Everyone called me J Roc. Within a few months after my release, I had everyone in my neighborhood gang banging. I had always wanted to fill my father's shoes, and now I

Chapter 1

was about that business. In my mind, I was built for this and people feared me, just like they did my dad. It felt great to have that power, and I fed on it and built quite a name for myself. I was all about action, quick to engage, applying gun play to any situation that I couldn't handle. Our entire clique was always quick to have a beef with anyone. Soon after all this, I discovered my drug of choice. It took me to a new place. All I can say is wow! For the first time ever, I loved being me. I loved how I felt. I didn't care what anyone thought of me. I thought I was experiencing heaven on earth. The drug seemed to make everything better. I would stay awake for days, robbing, fighting, and having sex for hours at a time. Drug use became my life. It Influenced my every decision. My thinking capacity was extremely limited. I became reckless and careless. By the time I was 17 years old, I had been arrested for indulging in criminal gang activity, initiating gang activity, and criminal misuse of a prohibited weapon.

I turned eighteen on my way to Varner Unit. This time I wasn't going to juvie; I was finally headed to the big time, the Arkansas Department

Jimmy McGill

of Corrections. It doesn't matter who you are or how tough you are, and it doesn't matter who you know in prison - regardless of how many friends or family members you have there, when it's your first ride down, you are terrified. I had heard nothing but war stories, and I was scared to death. But prison proved one thing to me—*I had nothing there to fear.*

Chapter 1

Chapter 2

Prison

Prison is literally a world inside of a world, a completely unimaginable culture. The first thing you learn when you walk through that gate is that everything you thought you knew was wrong. There are two separate factions that oversee every prison, and you had better learn both if you want to survive. On top of learning the rules and regulations enforced by the guards, you also must learn the *convict code*. Anyone hoping to leave prison intact must learn to keep everybody happy, both the inmate population and the correctional staff. One thing I learned really quickly was that I didn't know anything.

Chapter 2

There are only two types of people in prison, the ones who get by and those who don't. Life sucks there for everybody. Your unfortunate circumstances of how society did you wrong or how much time that you've got to face doesn't matter to the inmate population. The mindset of a convict is that "we're all doing bad." It is the one thing inmates share: we are in this cage together, but not together. Everybody deals with the same stress. The only difference between a killer and a petty thief is the will to survive. The only way you learn to live with the circumstances is to block out any hope of going home. You may have heard that old cliché that there are only two days that matter in prison, the day you arrive and the day you leave. Nothing could be further from the truth! Everything matters in prison! Every day matters! When you go to prison, that time is lost forever—you can't get that time back. *What you say today can get you killed tonight*; or, at the very least, really hurt. There is a lot you learn really quickly if you are going to make it in prison. You learn to be respectful to everybody, where and where not to eat, and even how to use the bathroom and shower without offending some-

Jimmy McGill

one else. The trickiest thing to learn is how and to whom to talk.

Talking in prison is a whole different ballgame than it is on the outside. There is definitely a proper prison jargon, and if you want to carry on a conversation without disrespecting a variety of different cultures and gang related people, you had better learn it. A simple word like "relative" may get your head split open. The slang that is spoken inside the prison walls is a language all to itself. If you're not careful, your conversation will lead to your demise without you even realizing what was happening. Basically, when you come into prison, regardless of how street smart you are, you must relearn everything you thought you knew. I had to set my values and principles in place. A man must know what he'll accept and what he won't, how far he is willing to be pushed and where to draw his "DO NOT CROSS" line.

In Arkansas on a *class B felony* or less, you do two months for every year you are sentenced. If you have a *class A felony*, you do fifty percent of your sentence, and on a *class Y felony*, you will serve seventy percent of your time. My sentence was light.

Chapter 2

I was given two years on a *B felony*. Theoretically I should have only served four months, and I did in prison; however, I spent nine months in the jail waiting to get to prison.

The whole time I was waiting to transfer to the prison system, everybody was telling me stories. I heard so many stories, and I couldn't decipher which ones were true and which ones were total falsehoods; after all, I had never been to the "big time." But almost all the stories had one person that always cropped up, for privacy reasons we'll call him Reggie Smith. Stay away from Uncle Reggie. He's a "booty bandit." I'll let you determine for yourself what that terminology means in a prison setting. They said Reggie had been in prison since prison was prison. They said he was a killer and a rapist. They said everybody inside the joint (prison system) needed to worry about him. By the time I arrived at Varner unit, I had heard so many stories about Reggie Smith that I expected him to be at least thirty feet tall, 650 pounds, and made of teflon. I figured he chewed up iron and pissed nails. One of the guys that I went through the diagnostics unit with said, "Jimmy, we're all scared; we just

Jimmy McGill

can't let nobody see it." One thing's for sure, what I feared the most was ever meeting Uncle Reggie.

When you are traveling to the state prison, you can see it from about a mile away. I'll never forget thinking it looked like a fortress, and really it was a fortress of sorts. When the prison came into sight, I think everybody on that bus with me who had never been to prison before had a gut wrench and an increased heart rate, and we started to sweat. I know that I was doing my best to pretend that I wasn't scared, but I was absolutely terrified. Regardless of how I was feeling on the inside, I walked slowly with my head held high and stood up straight. Of all the things that could have happened right off the bat, as we filed off the bus, I looked over to my right and saw a black man talking, chatting away with the officers. It was obvious that this was not his first rodeo and that he had been in prison for a long time. He was laughing and telling jokes with the guards just like he was one of them; he was completely at ease and comfortable. As I approached where he stood, I noticed his shirt read SMITH, R. My heart skipped a beat, and I thought OH, SH*T! The very person

Chapter 2

I never wanted to meet was the first person I met. He looked me straight in my face and said, "McGill, is Thomas your daddy?" My heart wanted to jump completely out of my chest. *The boogeyman was talking to me.* I nodded my head and said yes. He said, "Your daddy's a real killer; you'll be okay." I was terrified that it was a trick. I knew not to take gifts from anybody, including compliments, so I just nodded my head like a tough guy and went about my business; but I was literally scared to death. The entire time I was in prison, I never said anything else to Reggie, nor did he to me. Stories about what he was doing to other new inmates would travel down the hallways. I would pass him at chow call, but he would just glance and keep walking. I was grateful, to put it lightly. I guess I could thank my dad for that one; once again I was living in my father's world, riding in his shadow.

Shortly after I got to prison, I met a couple of convicted killers, Jessie Misskelley and Jason Baldwin. These were two of the three guys known as the "West Memphis Three," infamous for a triple-murder case out of West Memphis, Arkansas. They gained national attention from an HBO documentary, "Paradise Lost: The Child Murders at Robin Hood Hills," and were released from prison in 2011 after entering into an Alford plea. I actually liked Jessie; we slept beside each other in 1995 at Varner Unit. I didn't care too much for Jason. The day I got there, someone had just fought with him and put him in a neck brace. There was another murder case famous in Arkansas; the kid's name was Phillip Siegrist. They called him "Little Thirty" because the courts had given him a thirty-year prison sentence on a class Y felony. He was only about 14 years old when he got his sentence for a murder that the media labeled as "satanic." I ended up getting close to the guy over the years. Every time I returned to prison he was still there, and I have often wondered what became of him.

Evidently I carried myself like a standup guy. I did my best to adhere to all the advice my father had given me about prison. However, I just couldn't help from being an idiot from time to time. Two weeks after I made parole, I got into a fight with, of all things, a guy of another race, which is never a good idea, and over the TV, for Pete's sake. I was even the one who started it, and

Chapter 2

the whole thing could have been avoided if I had had a lick of sense. After the fight, we were both taken to the captain's office. But God in his mercy didn't let the situation revoke my parole. The captain looked at my jacket (my file) and said, "You've already made parole, and I'm not going to keep you here any longer, McGill," and sent me back to the barracks. For some unknown reason, the guy didn't bust me back. When I returned to the barracks, everybody had a new look of respect toward me. The people that I associated with told me that I "showcased on the guy," meaning that I won the fight. I was glad to know it.

I got out of prison with a new attitude, a bad one. My father was out of prison, and I was right there beside him for the first time in a long time. Immediately I began to distribute dope for him. I was also getting high. Everyone was getting high. It was cool to not have to hide it from my dad and not have to worry about him doing to me what he would do to other people if I messed up his money or used too much dope. I was the only thing he loved. Yet, he could only love me as much as he knew how to love. As I've said before, his percep-

Jimmy McGill

tion was twisted on what loving your child was supposed to look like.

By this time my drug use was progressing. As I sit here typing this, I can look back through time and see that my use started with Mad Dog 20/20 and then moved to marijuana. From there to methamphetamines and then to any other drug that I could get—cocaine, hydrocodone, narco, Valium, Xanax, and acid to name a few. I wasn't a picky drug addict; I wouldn't refuse a drug because it wasn't the one I was hoping to get. The truth is, I've seldom seen any person caught in addiction who will turn down a chemical of any sort.

As is the case with many addicts, I didn't think I had a problem. I didn't have a problem when I snorted it because I didn't smoke it; and when I started to smoke it, I didn't have a problem because I didn't shoot it. When I began to shoot it, I didn't have a problem because I didn't use dirty syringes. When I used a dirty syringe, I didn't have a problem because I didn't use it in front of kids. When I was diagnosed with hepatitis C, I didn't have a problem because it couldn't have been from drug use, it must have been unprotected sex. Ridiculous!

Chapter 2

There is a zero to three percent chance of getting hep C through sexual activity. I stayed in denial for a long time. The simple fact was that if there was somebody for me to compare my addiction to that appeared worse off than I was, then I never had a problem. I would compare, rationalize, and justify my use regardless of any evidence presenting itself that would highlight that I needed help.

In reality, I was trapped in the grip of addiction. My drug use was the driving force of my life; nothing else really mattered. I had become my father, just maybe not as strategic. I would love to blame drugs for taking everything away from me, but I'm a realist—and I know that the hard truth is that I gave it all away. Somewhere along the way, I made a decision to either be a victim or a volunteer. I always knew the difference between right and wrong. My decisions were what destroyed me, and God is the one who has rebuilt me. Granted, my childhood was less than nurturing and obviously played into my decisions; nonetheless, they were *my* decisions. There really wasn't anything I wouldn't give up for the feeling I got when I put that chemical inside my body. I made terrible, irrational deci-

Jimmy McGill

sions, and my addiction led me down the path of destruction and landed me in prison six different times.

Using drugs definitely did not make me smarter. Seriously, I was probably one of the stupidest criminals in Arkansas. Once I was in pursuit of finding a way to get high but had no money in my pocket, so I burglarized a house and stole a rare set of Jap-animation cartoon movies. I took them to a Hastings bookstore because I knew that they would buy DVDs for a couple of dollars each. I handed the store clerk the DVDs and waited on my money. He skimmed through them and said, "Hey, I've got this movie," and he turned to the next one and he said, "I've got this one too." Then he looked at the third disk, and glancing up at me asked, "Sir, can I ask you where you got these?" I immediately got defensive and replied, "They're mine, why?" He replied, "Hang on, I've got to call my house." I ran out as fast I could run and got away that day. Out of all the houses that I could've robbed and all the Hastings stores to which I could have tried to sell my merchandise, I had broken into that store manager's house and tried to sell him his own DVDs. Like

Chapter 2

I said, I would have never qualified for the world's most intuitive criminal.

Although I didn't realize it at the time, looking back I believe God had His eye on me that day, and He had decided that He was going to catch up with me and was going to use Captain Kirk Lane to do it. Funny how God was always doing for me the things that I couldn't do for myself, like keeping me alive.

I had heard of Captain Lane by then, but I had always been able to avoid him. He was head over the Criminal Investigation Division (CID) of the Pulaski County Sheriff's Office, which meant that he had all of the detectives and narcotic officers under his lead. But I didn't care if he had the Army! I was going to get my hit of dope! None of them would get me, uh-uh, not Jimmy. Never mind the fact that everyone from my side of the tracks ran at the sound of his name. The old heads told plenty of stories about him. He had a reputation of always getting his guy! I had yet to be arrested by him; however, that would soon change. After I pulled the Hastings stunt, his detectives picked me up, and I got a seven-year prison sentence over it.

Jimmy McGill

This was my second or third trip to prison; I can't rightly remember. I had no way of knowing this at the time of my arrest, but as I was feeling all mad at the world, God was actually working out my future. Meeting Kirk was God laying the groundwork for what would later become the most amazing adventure of my life. I could not have even dreamed up the future God had in store for me.

This prison stint didn't scare me like the first time up. It was now kind of a lifestyle for me. Both the streets and prison are full snakes, and I was comfortable in a snake den. People that have never walked this path might have a hard time understanding how one can be so at home in such an environment. The answer is simple. Someone can't want a life they don't even know exists. This reptilian world was all I had ever known. It was my normal. Heck, when your own dad beats the crap out of you and pretty much abandons you to your own devices, what do you expect from the rest of the world?

By this time I was awfully familiar with prison life. As I stated earlier, prison is a vastly different world from the "outside." In prison the measure-

Chapter 2

ment of importance is viewed very differently. Homeless people previously trapped in addiction can become secure and stable. A few packs of TOP Tobacco can turn someone into a thousand-dollar baller. Although, I have to add, cigarettes can get you into all kinds of trouble in prison. I stayed in a mess because of smoking. I received write-ups and spent my time in the hole all for trafficking tobacco.

Even though prison was a miserable place where I was supervised by people I couldn't stand, there were times that I had fun. Believe it or not, I laughed harder in prison than I'd ever laughed on the streets. After all, I was experiencing long-time lengths of sobriety. Of course, the sense of humor of somebody that's doing a prison sentence is obviously going to be different from that of a normal, productive member of society. What I thought was funny, you probably would have thought insane. One example of our warped sense of humor was when we sold a short hair horse manure as marijuana. When new inmates arrive in prison, they are called short hairs, implying that they're new to the system. They don't know the ropes, the lingo,

Jimmy McGill

or the game. The short hairs go into intake barracks. They stay in the intake barracks between thirty and sixty days; then they are moved down the hallway where the oldies stay. It's very easy to take advantage of a short hair. They get tormented and taken advantage of for everything from financial situations to sexual favors. Well, this particular short hair wanted to buy a dime sack of weed. He came down the hallway to get it, and instead of weed we sold him horse poop. To us, that was funny enough, but then he came back a second time and wanted more. We sold him horse poop again and laughed so hard that our stomachs hurt. While laughing, we enjoyed his twenty dollars at the commissary. Poor guy! We could not wrap our minds around how in the world someone could smoke horse poop twice and be so happy.

The following picture was in the height of my underground music career. I was doing time in Pulaski County jail for a parole violation. I was waiting to go back to prison, again. It was the fourth or fifth time, I think. My parole officer picked me up for a music video that I had made that had guns in the video. This picture was taken by my manager

Chapter 2

Brad. His nickname was Dirty, and he was trying to keep my buzz built up so that when I was doing time I would still have a musical following when I came home. Hopefully I could still do shows and sell music once I was released. So, of course, I had to be hard in the picture, displaying a thug image and flipping off the camera. I still have no idea how he got the phone through visitation, but he did.

The next picture was taken by a fan. I was sitting in Jacksonville city jail on an arrest for possession of a controlled substance. I was actually making bond at the time this picture was taken.

Jimmy McGill

McGill in Prison

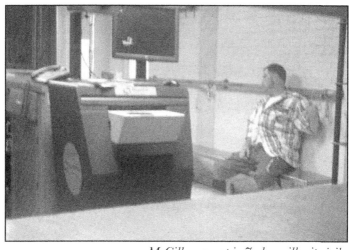

McGill on arrest in Jacksonville city jail

Chapter 2

Chapter 3

Addiction

Although I spent most of my life in and out of jails and prisons, my real prison started way before the incarceration of my body. My real prison, the prison in my own mind, began when I was incredibly young and continued for years. The Arkansas Department of Corrections was a cakewalk compared to the self-imposed mental prison of my drug addiction. Today I see the insanity of my lifestyle. For me, my addiction did not begin with a chemical substance. My gateway drug was trauma. You need to understand that I scored a ten on the Adverse Childhood Experiences (ACE) test. If you don't know what that is, google it. Childhood

Chapter 3

trauma left me never feeling that I was enough. I mentioned before that the first thing I ever used to change the way I felt was attention. I cared so deeply what others thought of me. In pursuit of trying to make other people like me, I did what everyone around me was doing—used drugs. This led me in and out of incarceration multiple times and was part of what fed my mental prison. Drugs did not bring me clarity of mind by any stretch of the imagination. One sentence I received was completely due to my inability to think properly because my mind was in a drug fog. I had broken into a house with a couple of guys, and while they were loading up the car, I decided that it was a great time to take a smoke break. So, I lit up a cigarette under the people's carport. Bad idea! The residents who lived there did not smoke, so when I thumped my cigarette butt under their carport, I did not consider the fact that the police would possibly run my DNA from the cigarette butt. Even I felt stupid over that one.

When I was finally released from that prison sentence, I went straight after the thing that I had been obsessing on every day of my incarceration, *a*

Jimmy McGill

shot of dope.

There are two components that make up all addiction, and they are obsession and compulsion. A mental obsession and a physical compulsion that is driven by an overwhelming desire to use that ends in insanity. My actions and behavior in my effort to go to any length to get high is the evidence of my insanity. I was a total cuckoo bird. When a person is in addiction, getting and using the drug becomes the only thing that matters to them. That desire outweighs any moral principle that person ever had. It literally takes over the mind, and the drug becomes the driving force of life. People put their lives in jeopardy every day for the sake of getting high. Breaking into places is commonplace for someone in a life of addiction. It was such normal behavior for us that we would refer to it as doing chores—you know, cleaning house.

You have heard that the definition of insanity is doing the same thing over and over again but expecting a different result. In addiction this may be true, but it goes much deeper. The insanity that accompanies the disease of addiction rivals candidacy for a mental institution. This is the type of

Chapter 3

insanity that will have you getting high in the parole office parking lot, knowing that you are about to receive a drug test. Picture this: You've already been told you will be getting drug screened. You get high and walk in the building hoping for a miracle—that your parole officer may not be there, or that they might forget they were going to test you, or that maybe for some reason you might accidentally pass the test. Like I said, insanity.

Addiction leads you places you never imagined you would find yourself. For me this meant being a deadbeat father, a terrible person, a manipulator, a liar, a thief, and a thug. I was neglecting God, personal hygiene, future plans, and basically everything. Truly, I stopped living. People in addiction push responsibility to the side. Children no longer matter; life really is no longer a priority. The drug use is the only thing that matters.

There is a misconception that people in addiction use drugs because we like them. This could not be further from the truth. We use because, in that moment, we cannot function or live life without them. I did things so shameful in pursuit of using that it hurts to think about them to this very day. I have accidentally shot up bleach because I was in such a hurry to do the shot. I was using a dirty syringe and cleaning it with bleach. The bleach made me feel safe and like I wasn't completely helpless and powerless. I was moving in too much of a hurry and put the bleach on the dope instead of the water. I had no idea that I had accidentally mixed bleach and dope until it was too late. The second the plunger hit the syringe, I felt the heat of the dope and instantly tasted the bleach. That taste dominated my throat. Trust me, bleach tastes as strong as it smells. I spent a few minutes in a paranoid state of mind. I had an overwhelming fear that I had just done something I couldn't take back and that I was going to die or had severely messed up my body, but after an hour passed by and I was still alive, the thoughts slowly disappeared.

I have also used Mountain Dew, ditch water, and toilet water to do dope with when there was no tap water available; nothing could stop the obsession. I was like something off *The Walking Dead*—a zombie. The sad thing about this is that I thought I looked great. I literally believed that I was "as fly as

Chapter 3

an airplane."

Cravings are a mental obsession for drugs. I really have no words to explain the power of cravings. Cravings throw you into a constant state of misery. I look back on myself in my addiction, and I see the insanity of it all. I was so controlled by my mental obsession to the point that I couldn't even enjoy my high, because I would start worrying about my next one. I can't count the number of times that I did a shot of dope that I knew was not going to get me high—I mean, it didn't even have to be a drug—holding on to hope and sheer desperation that I would feel it. When the drug hit my arm, it was like instant perversion. I can remember taking things apart that were brand new for no reason at all. I would putter around in the same room tweaking things for hours, never coming out, no shower, no toothbrush, just stuck on stupid. I guess I thought that magically something different would somehow appear in the room. There were times my friends and I spent six or seven hours straight trying to untangle a box of phone chargers, all the while tangling them worse as we went. The saddest part of this was that I was not alone. Everyone I

Jimmy McGill

knew suffered in the same demented mindset.

Addiction messes up your thinking. Paranoia is the name of the game. I constantly thought everyone was talking about me. I just knew they were all plotting my demise or trying to get something from me. I can remember digging through trash for hours, looking for hidden notes or messages between the people that were around me. I saw messages written on the tile in the shower, in ink that was designed to blend in with the wall. Pure insanity! I lived with a continual sense that I was missing out on something, that everyone else knew about something and I was being excluded. I felt that others were embarrassed by having me around. It didn't matter that I was broke with nothing in my pocket, not even a drug; everyone in my realm was conspiring against me. It was impossible to have a normal relationship with a woman because as soon as I got high, I would think that absolutely everyone I knew was sleeping with her. If we were together and I used, I would badger the poor woman for hours with tedious questions and suspicions. I would think that she was trying to intentionally make me look like a fool and steal what little I

Chapter 3

could hustle to share with all these imaginary people. Any woman with whom I would try to have a relationship would end up hating me.

Most people stay in addiction for so long because they are in denial that they have a problem. Part of denial is blaming others and refusing to take personal responsibility. When I was in addiction, I would always blame someone else for my actions and their consequences; nothing was ever my fault. The way I saw it, I didn't need help as long as I could rationalize or justify the situation. None of the consequences in my life were my fault; I would always find a way to blame someone else for the current problem or crisis. For example, when sitting in jail on a parole violation for a failed drug test, I remember being angry with the parole officer for drug testing me. It was all his fault that I was in jail at that moment; never mind that I was non-compliant with my parole stipulations. *If the parole officer had not drug tested me, then I wouldn't be here.* Like I said, nothing was ever my fault, and I did not have a drug problem. After all, I could always look to someone much worse off than myself.

Addiction demands that a person is completely

Jimmy McGill

self-centered. How the other person feels or what he or she needs or wants doesn't matter. All that matters is that I get what I want, when I want it, and the way I want it. When an addict doesn't like the way he or she feels, then the entire focus is on changing that feeling by any means necessary. In my experience most of the people I met in my addiction were also in their addictions. We all behaved like children. We were very selfish and very inconsiderate and would lie, cheat, and steal to get what we needed.

They say that once you start using drugs, the human brain stops developing. I believe this to be true. In the last five years, I have matured more than in all my other 38 years of life. My process of recovery began the healing of my mind, body, and spirit. Because I spent so much of my life dedicated to selfishness, I now spend most of my time trying to be selfless and to help others. Being of service to other people is my way of giving back for all that I've taken. I found my new purpose in helping people who are still sick. At the core of addiction is self-centeredness, so being of service to other people goes against everything the disease demanded

Chapter 3

of me. It is my greatest insurance policy against returning to drug use.

According to The American Society of Addiction Medicine (ASAM), addiction is a chronic brain disorder and not simply a behavioral problem involving too much alcohol, drugs, gambling, or sex. In addiction the brain basically rewires itself into a pleasure and reward system. It's quite simple. If you add a drug, any drug, to the condition of experiencing pain, humiliation, hurt, despair, embarrassment, or any other negative feeling, it equals relief. Over time our brains readjust to that equation. As I talked about before, my childhood was full of pain, embarrassment, loneliness, and humiliation. I had been neglected, bullied, and abused in every way—emotionally, verbally, and sexually. I never felt "good enough" for everyone else. I continually sought to change the way I felt. Drugs were my solution to all of my problems. They were my chosen vice and allowed me the opportunity to escape the reality of my life. But then they took over my life. In the beginning, my drug use was social, but like all addiction the use became progressive. I was unable to see the line

Jimmy McGill

when I crossed it. Looking back, that crossover is still blurry as to when my using went from casual to daily dependency.

I know this about addiction—it is fatal, progressive, and incurable. My addiction started with one initial drug use and became an uncontrollable necessity to my existence. I had a brain that wanted me to believe it could continue to live even if my body died. Addiction is a disease of perception—you try to convince yourself that you do not have a problem. As an addict, you cling to the thought that you're just like everyone else. This is a disease that leads you to think you don't have a disease. Addiction does not discriminate based on age, gender, race, sexuality, or morals, and it does not have guidelines. Anyone can be affected by the disease. I had something wired differently in my mind that would not let me stop with just one of anything. Anything that makes me feel good has the potential to be addictive.

An addict has no boundaries. At the end of the night, when everybody else goes to sleep and the party dies down, the addict will be left awake, searching through the couch cushions for a bag,

Chapter 3

looking in the ashtrays for a roach (butt-end of a joint), looking for a dropped pill on the floor, or trying to find a bottle someone left half drunk. At six a.m., when everyone's getting up for class, the true addict will still be pilfering, trying to find a drug to use. This was the difference between me and my friends.

So, give me just a minute to speak the truth to anyone who can relate to what I've been describing. If you're trying to escape your pain, and you think that a drug will change the way you feel, that it will take away your sadness, your embarrassment, and your hurt, you are absolutely correct. However, it will also take away your feelings, your ability to think and make decisions. It'll take away your family, your children, and all of your morals and values. It will take your job, car, house, your health, and anything else that you've gotten. You need to realize the insanity of thinking that putting a chemical inside your body can ever change the circumstances surrounding you. When the induced euphoria is gone, the circumstances will remain the same. Actually, they will have probably gotten worse because while high you have neglected your

Jimmy McGill

responsibility a little longer and have amplified your original problem. The misery that comes from addiction becomes comfortable and familiar. For years it was my closest companion. Experiencing the emotional pain of my addiction was the only thing I could count on even though I hated myself because I couldn't stop. Yet, I simply couldn't see the problem.

Chapter 3

Chapter 4

Cracker Swagger

Somewhere around 2006 on one of my jail stints, I decided to become a rapper. Crazy, huh? I went a lot further with it than one might think. During my bid (a bid is a prison sentence that you have to serve), there was a guy locked up named Cortez. He was a rapper. He loved to make music, and we would beat on the window in the rec yard for hours at time. He would rap for the whole unit. We would gather around him, and even though we were in jail, we would be having a concert and would find freedom through that music. You could say that we were captivated in captivity by his voice and his music. Every day he would beat on

Chapter 4

that window and he would perform for us, and we would temporarily be released from our cages. He rapped so amazingly that it inspired me, a guy with no musical talent, to try it myself. So during the remaining time of my incarceration, I wrote rhymes.

Although I couldn't really ride a beat, the lyrics were great. I liked rapping so much that I continued to pursue it once I was released. I came home and found a recording studio, walked in, and started laying down music tracks. I had a few good songs.

Sara Merritt believed in my music from the beginning. She was both my lawyer and my best friend. She made her way into dozens of my songs. I prided myself on rapping about my life. The pistol play, the dope game, my lawyer. I lived with Sara for ten years. She believed in me to the point of financially backing my music career. She bankrolled me from studio time to CD production and distribution. She was president of the Criminal Defense Attorneys Association in Arkansas, and with my network of criminal friendships, she was constantly booming in her law business. Every time someone I knew got arrested, I would

Jimmy McGill

refer them to Sara. We were living a lifestyle of the rich and famous, and I was rapping about it. She even tattooed our first studio on her leg! I felt bulletproof with Sara. The police would pick me up, and she would walk me out of the police station like a boss on a gangster movie. The next day the incident was the inspiration for a new track. Sara and I would stay for days at the casinos. Once she suggested that I be a professional gambler. We spent thousands a week in the casinos, and we won thousands. I remember once I hit three hand-pay jackpots in the same night. Then as we walked out, we stopped at the crap table and I won another $1,600. She casually sat down at the penny slot beside the dice table, and she hit for a $1,200 jackpot. Sara's daughter, Mary Scarlett, and I did a track together that is still one of my favorites today.

One thing I was good at was promotion. With social media it didn't take long to learn that music was about twenty percent skill and eighty percent one's ability to put oneself out there to get known. I started on Myspace and then went to Facebook, Twitter, and other social media sites. I started shooting videos and learning how to edit videos. I

Chapter 4

ended up being surprisingly good at it. I traveled around to several states doing shows. Sara paid for my first video. She always saw something in me nobody else could see. After that I knew I should learn how to produce my own videos, and I did. I also made a ton of videos. Some were bootleg garbage, but others were high quality and great. I made good friends along the way. Sometimes I would be clean from drugs and sometimes not so much. One thing I learned: being high on meth and trying to perform on stage was a horrible combination. Trying to rap while watching the crowd because of a drug-induced psychosis causing total paranoia was terrible. I remember trying to watch the girl that I was with, thinking she was in the crowd doing stuff with other guys. Pure insanity.

Most of my music career took place in Savannah, Georgia. I started making music in Little Rock, but like the scripture says, "No prophet is accepted in his own hometown." People always "hated on" what I was doing in Little Rock. Sara and I opened our first legitimate studio, Criminal Element Music Productions, which was across the street from her law office. We basically threw that

Jimmy McGill

money down the drain because I was too high to ever produce any good music out of that studio. If we could turn back time and I could have stayed sober, we would both be millionaires. But then my purpose would not be what it is today. Once I moved, as the years went by, my talent got better. I learned to ride a beat and how to deliver my lyrics. I strengthened my network. I also learned to talk noise (trash talk, crack jokes, get my front on, etc.), which helped a lot. I'm a crap talker and I can often be a joker, so I began making blog videos. Kind of like a "YouTuber," except this was before YouTube was popular. I began to make roast videos. I would talk about anyone or anything. A lot of Nashville rappers started taking notice of what I was doing in Savannah including Jelly Roll, Haystak, Struggle, and Worm, so I formed light relationships with them. I teamed up with Kyle Hinton, Yard Call, and he still makes music today. We became brothers and spent most of our time in the recording booth. I met Yard Call during my first trip back to Savannah to reunite with my foster mom. Somehow Sara had arranged a visit between my mother and myself. It had been 17 years

Chapter 4

since I had seen Linda, and somehow Sara had tracked her down and we had flown down there for my birthday. We had dinner at Ruth's Chris. I invited Yard Call over so that I could meet him and we could go to the studio. When he walked in, he was completely the opposite of anything that I possibly could have imagined. I was thinking he was a gang banger like me. Nope! LOL! He was 6'5", 350 pounds. He had to turn sideways to walk through the door, and his hair was down to the middle of his back. He was a long-haired hippie boy with a southern twang in his voice, but man, could he rap. The first time we went to the studio we recorded a song called "Full Blooded Goon." It was hands down the best song either of us had ever recorded. It was our favorite. In fact, it was a favorite of almost anyone we let hear it. We did shows in Tennessee, Arkansas, Georgia, and Florida. Sometimes they were big shows; sometimes they were exceedingly small shows. We never knew what we were going to get because we never knew who was promoting our concert. I never imagined Kyle and I would be the friends that we still are today. We don't see each other often, but we talk now and

Jimmy McGill

then. I'll get a message from him out of nowhere telling me how proud he is of me.

I eventually moved to Savannah, Georgia with my mother, started college, and stayed clean on my own for a while. Since Yard Call and I both lived in Savannah now, making music was easier. I found a club that was willing to let Yard Call and me perform on a regular basis. And so we started having a regular hip-hop night in Savannah. It didn't take me long to mix common sense with business. The more people you get involved, the more you cross tap into each other's following and fanbases. The longer Yard Call and I made music, the better we got, and the more people who came on board. Before we knew it, we had created a movement and underground management team called Street Swagg Family, and everywhere we went everybody was representing it. I started building a reputation and making my brand known in Savannah. Lil Wyte told me the best thing that I could do was to have a name that was unique and fit me. I became J Bo Cracker Swagger.

I found a management/promotions contract on the internet and downloaded and tweaked it to

Chapter 4

fit Street Swagg Family. I began recruiting other underground artists in Savannah, Arkansas, and Tennessee. They would pay me $100 management fee and sign the contract. They could say that they were part of Street Swagg Family and would immediately get the same attention J Bo Cracker Swagger and Yard Call were getting. They were also able to perform at places we performed. I was hustling the music scene the same way I did the dope game, getting over on anyone that I could and making a dollar any way I could.

I wasn't scared to fight and considered myself a gangster, so the image of a street life rapper came easily to me. There were times I jumped off the concert stage and got into fights, but that really wasn't good for business because after that we usually didn't get another booking. I remember Yard Call got in a fight one night, and one of the fans ran in the building as I was performing and yelled "Yard Call is fighting!" I came flying off the stage arms swinging. That was a big night for us—we were performing with Lil Wyte, a Memphis, Tennessee rapper who found his fame and fortune through the Triple Six Mafia.

Jimmy McGill

I have songs with Bubba Sparxxx and Big Smo. I've had concerts with some of the hottest underground rappers around. At one point in my life, I thought I was surely destined to make music forever. We were getting bigger and bigger; however, this was not to be. I had no idea that was God setting the stage for a bigger platform for me.

Not long after this climb, I experienced a trauma that caused me to leave Georgia, spiral out of control in my addiction, and give up any hope of making music. I was performing at a club in Rincon, Georgia, and my mother was killed instantly in a car wreck while leaving that concert. This was very painful for me. I had been somewhat sober during this season, but experiencing a pain that I did not know how to handle just sent me into my default mode—using. I stayed numb through it all. That's what the dope did for me; it numbed me. It would be almost a decade later, as part of my recovery process, before I would finally grieve the loss of my mother.

After my mother's death, I only did a couple of big concerts. The concerts were called "Crunkfest," and Haystak and I were the main perform-

Chapter 4

ers; but honestly I could not keep a syringe out of my arm long enough to continue pursuing music. Like all things in my addiction, the microphone took the backseat. Dope became the priority; music was secondary, and in my pursuit to constantly stay high that dream was lost.

J Bo and Jelly Roll in Little Rock, AR 2016

Jimmy McGill

J Bo and Lil Wyte in Savannah, GA 2011

J Bo in Little Rock, AR 2012 Crunkfest 2

Chapter 4

J Bo and Haystack in Little Rock, AR 2012 Crunkfest 3

J Bo and Yard Call The Rutledge in Nashville, TN 2010 | Photo credit @ RoseWood Photography

Jimmy McGill

J Bo and Scrap in Nashville, TN

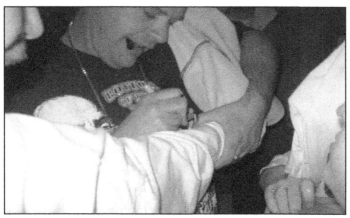

J Bo signing a fan's arm in Kansas City

Chapter 4

J Bo with a friend from prison at Juanita's Show in Little Rock, AR
2016

Jimmy McGill

J Bo with foster mom, Linda, at Tybee Island, GA

Chapter 4

Video shoot with Oddball

Chapter 5

Recovery

Recovery is different for everyone. Although the nature of our pathways may be similar, we will each have quite different experiences during the process. There are many approaches to recovery. Some people recover through a twelve-step program; others use SMART recovery, or natural recovery. There are those who strictly use church and a personal relationship with God. Still others may use CrossFit and exercise. Some people maintain long-term recovery out of sheer desperation to never return to the pain and misery of drug use. Regardless of your personal journey, you will find that you will need a daily dose of whichever

Chapter 5

method you have chosen if you want to achieve long-term recovery. The disease of addiction is not curable. It exists seven days a week; therefore, recovery must exist seven days a week.

There is no such thing as successful "part-time" recovery. If exercise and church is your thing, then I suggest you exercise and pray daily. If you're a twelve-stepper and find relief and freedom through the twelve steps, then I suggest you go to a meeting daily or at least most of the week. If you go to a self-help group four days a week and then do nothing to support your recovery for the remaining three days, then you have in fact given most of your week to recovery but three days of it to the disease. For a person who suffers with the disease of addiction, you are either recovering or you're on your way back to addiction.

A common misconception that is often heard about recovery is that *"relapse is part of recovery."* This is not true! Relapse is part of the disease. The disease of addiction is the problem; recovery itself is the solution. Therefore, if relapse is the problem it cannot be part of the solution. Relapse is the nature of the disease but not necessary for a person to sustain recovery. I have been blessed on my personal journey. Thus far, five years into my recovery, relapse has not been a part of my story. I pray daily that it never will be. I know people who have never relapsed that have thirty *consecutive* years of recovery. Relapse is not a prerequisite for recovery; it's a choice, a decision that someone makes with a clear mind, usually because they've stopped their daily maintenance in some form or fashion.

Medically **A**ssisted **T**reatment (MAT)

I support the scientific, evidence-based findings of the practice of medically assisted recovery. I have close friends who are in long-term recovery, and their sobriety was found through the process of Suboxone use. So I know it works. However, there are many prescribers who think that just slinging you a buprenorphine and naloxone combination without any services paired with the prescription is the answer, and that is simply ridiculous. This aggravates me to my core. Although it would be nice, there is no pill that can cure addiction. MAT can be part of long-term, sustainable results when it is coupled with recovery support, but if a person is just given a Suboxone prescription and not offered recovery support, then the addict is simply changing substances and not learning the responsibility of true recovery. This is why the recovery community tends to stigmatize medically-assisted treatment. It's bad enough that normal society (normies) places stigma on people recovering from addiction, but now, recovering people are contributing to the stigma as well. Again, I'm not against MAT as one part of a recovery program. I am against it as a program in and of itself.

It's closed-minded to think that my pathway to recovery is the only working pathway for all people. Just because one way didn't work for me doesn't mean that it won't work for you. Personally, I believe that there are many good people in the medical field trying to save lives and help their patients to overcome the battle against addiction. However, I believe it would be beneficial if the medical community would become more informed about addiction recovery. We would see better results. As people in long-term recovery, we have a great opportunity to open dialogue about recovery with these medical professionals. Who better to advocate for recovery than the people who are walking the path themselves? Research shows the more successful Suboxone clinics tend to offer peer recovery support services. They have peer specialists working in their clinics. A peer recovery specialist is someone with **<u>DIRECT</u>** lived experience in recovery from their own addiction. Most of the time they have a minimum of two years of sustained recovery. Some states have a lesser time requirement. Peers understand the addiction recovery and the disease. They understand the recovery processes, and they have been trained and credentialed. A peer walks *with* the individual seeking recovery and is so effective in the recovery field because of his or her ability to identify with the sick and suffering person in addiction.

In my addiction there were a lot of professional people who were overqualified to provide services to me. They were counselors, therapists, psychologists, preachers, teachers, and mental health professionals. They were probably great at their jobs. Had I been willing to let them, I'm sure they could have helped me. They weren't the problem; I was. I was not willing to open up and be honest with any of them. I feared they would judge me, and I

Chapter 5

was afraid they would be condescending to me. I didn't want to tell them the truth, that I was a liar and a thief, that I stole everything my mother had, that I've been molested, that I had sexually acted out. I didn't want to say any of these things because of how they might look at me. However, with peer recovery, the fear of judgment is completely removed. When it was another person in recovery standing in front of me, reaching out and offering to help me, they were able to accomplish in a matter of moments what all these professional people had never been able to accomplish.

When I was introduced to someone with lived experience, I was inspired to be honest and open up. I was willing to trust; we had an instant rapport. I knew I wouldn't be judged for doing the same things the person speaking to me had done; heck, maybe they had done even worse things. The peers that worked with me were authentic and transparent. They had a sincere desire to help because they had been where I was and were empathetic to my plight. They understood me and I knew it. In a matter of moments, I knew that they understood the self-imposed mental prison I was experiencing, that they had felt the same misery, shame, guilt, and remorse that marked my mind; yet in spite of it all, they were successfully living life. They were no longer victims of circumstances. They were products of their own decisions. I wanted that! It was after spending time with a peer that I realized for the first time that hope was possible. A peer changed my perception in minutes. That is the power of lived experience.

Recovery is an amazing thing! It is where someone finds a purpose from a past full of mistakes and hurt. The process of recovery will take someone out of a lifetime of addiction, misery, and prison, and turn that into a pathway and purpose. ***People can and do recover***. Regardless of the pathway we choose, we can lose the desire to pick up and use. The second we realize that we have a choice and we never have to get high again—well, it's a game changer. The ultimate weapon to combat addiction is one recovering person helping another; nothing is as effective and powerful for recovery.

The first ninety days of recovery is usually when new people in recovery make all of our idiotic mis-

Chapter 5

takes. I was definitely no exception to the rule. The beginning of my recovery was risky, dangerous, and stupid, not to mention illegal.

My early recovery was definitely a rollercoaster ride, to say the least. I had one foot in recovery and one foot still in the street. I had just been released from prison for the sixth time, and I had no idea if I was going to stay clean or go back to my old life. I still had a pending drug charge, and in my mind, I knew I was going to get a large prison sentence whenever I went back to court. It was sheer luck that I was accepted into the chem-free house (a sober living home) to which they allowed me to parole. There were sixty people residing there. Only four of them were allowed to be parolees. Keep in mind that out of all six trips to the Department of Corrections, this was the first time I did something different when I made parole. Instead of going back to the same toxic environments that I'd always been released to, I went somewhere different. I had no idea what to expect! I was nervous and just went with the flow. I had no clue that I would hear a message of hope and find a new way to live.

My first ninety days out of prison this time

showed that I was unsure but hopeful. I did well when it came to staying clean; however, I was living dirty. The life I had always lived was the only life I'd known. I quickly began to make friends with the staff and directors, and I used this rapport to my benefit. One of my friends from the streets had a pending drug charge and was facing prison time. I was able to sweet talk the facility into accepting him into the program. Once he moved in, it took no time at all to get him moved to my room. Here we go!! Two neighborhood boys living the same lifestyle with the same mindset in the same room. Twenty-four hours later, I had a bag of dope and was selling it out of my residential living facility.

I was on fire for recovery, and I somehow thought that I could sell but not use. Because of my criminal history, I couldn't find employment. I needed to pay my phone bill and my weekly rent at my chem-free place. I needed cigarettes and food, so I rationalized and convinced myself that as long as I stayed clean I could still hustle. Today I know how selfish, stupid, and reckless that was, and I only stayed clean through all of that by the grace of God. The first twelve weeks that I was in the

Chapter 5

chem-free home, I would take my weekend passes at the trap house with a girl I used to date before prison. I would lay up with her all weekend while she hustled and sold my dope. I would take the money back to chem-free, get caught up on all my bills, and continue to search for work. I still can't believe I stayed clean. My roommate (who shall remain nameless) got romantically involved with the staff member at the front desk of the center. So we had inside information about everything going on. She would later lose her job because of him.

Even though I was not living a clean lifestyle, I was sober. So every time I went to a meeting, I heard the message a little more clearly. It wasn't long until I began believing that people could stay clean and find a new way to live. I started really trying to dig into the recovery literature, and I was doing what my sponsor (another person in long-term recovery who guides you through your process) was telling me to do. The change came suddenly and quickly. The day I bought into recovery all the way is a day I will never forget. It was a Saturday night, and I had been asleep when my roommate came in. Weekend curfew was midnight, and I had gone to sleep early. When I woke up Sunday morning, he was already awake looking at me in an incredibly nervous manner. His body language was somewhere between paranoia and fear. He said, "I couldn't stop and stash this in time to make it in by curfew." He pointed to a newspaper that was spread out on his bed. The newspaper had a large hump, and I knew instantly that there was something under it. He peeled the newspaper back like he was revealing a prize, and there it was staring me right in the face: A LIFE SENTENCE.

He had a pistol and a pound of methamphetamine inside of our bedroom. Immediately God showed to me the stupidity of my choices. From that second on, there's been no looking back. I made a phone call and had someone come pick him up and get the dope and the gun out of our room. I've been 110% bought into recovery, and I've never put my recovery at risk nor broken the law since.

Like everyone with a history as colorful as mine, I struggled to find employment. I would hire on for temporary agencies or for friends who knew people that needed help here and there, but even though

Chapter 5

times were hard and selling dope would have been easy money, I didn't go back and I didn't get high. I began to work my recovery just as seriously as I had my addiction. I did this by digging into recovery literature and working the twelve steps. I started unpacking a lifetime of childhood trauma that had never been addressed. The longer I stayed clean, the more I began to enjoy life. I was listening to people, trying new things, and doing my best to be humble and open minded. A closed mind cannot graft a new idea. Recovery—for an addict like me—is a brand-new idea.

About four months into my chem-free, my cousin Jennifer Ziggler did something that really impacted my life. Jennifer had been clean three years at the time, and she made recovery fun and appealing. She was my inspiration. She really influenced my early recovery like no other. I had nine months clean when she picked up her three-year key tag. That was her three-year birthday of going without using drugs at all, and that birthday tag is special to anyone in recovery. She did the most selfless thing that I had ever experienced in my life at that time. She took her birthday key tag and called me up for it and gave it to me, and she told me that on the day I get my three-year tag to make sure I give it away. Three years seem like a long time from nine months, but I'll be damned if I didn't get a three-year key tag and give it away.

Jennifer and I had thousands of conversations on everything that I would encounter in life over my first two years of living clean. Whenever I would have an epiphany about recovery, I would call and share it with her. Whenever I had a question, I would call and ask her. If I needed experience, strength, or hope, I would call Jen and we would burn that telephone up. She was my rock. It wasn't long after that I began taking my step work and my recovery meetings to a different level. I was putting my everything into it.

I met my best friend Matt in my chem-free; we were polar opposites and didn't like each other at all. If you were to tell me this guy was going to end up being my best friend and a groomsman at my wedding, I would've thought you were cuckoo.

Matt grew up completely different from the way I did. He went to Catholic High and had good parents. Matt was a good kid who should never have

Chapter 5

had to experience addiction. Matt hurt his shoulder from a football injury and received a prescription to get through the pain. That prescription is what began a lifetime heroin addiction. Eventually, after hundreds of smart-ass remarks and foul comments being exchanged between Matt and me, mostly during our daily groups at our chemical-free residence, we became friends. I still don't know how it happened. Somewhere, in the midst of the sarcasm, we found a common bond in our desire to stay clean, and we slowly started hanging around each other. I had no idea how to have a friendship. Matt and I would learn together.

When I had about fourteen months clean, I began college. I enrolled at Pulaski Tech College, which is part of the University of Arkansas. Matt would get up every morning, even on his off days, and drive me to school. In an attempt to be humble, I rode the bus a few times. However, it surely triggered my addiction. There would be homeless people in the back of the bus talking about drug use, discussing how they were fixing to go cop somebody a sack (buy drugs); it was just an unhealthy environment for me. I couldn't do the bus rides.

Those morning car rides with Matt would become the foundation of our friendship. Matt and I are still extremely close today. Through Matt's recovery, he went on to become a manager of one of the Cheddar's restaurants in Little Rock. He gives a lot of newcomers (people new in recovery) a job. That is his way of giving back. We FaceTime and we talk. We see each other in meetings and at recovery conventions. Most importantly, we make time for each other to meet and have a "bro day."

By the time I had eighteen months clean, you couldn't get me to shut up, not about recovery. It was the only thing I talked about. I was excited and happy. I needed the world to know that an addict like me was living clean.

I was being asked to share my recovery everywhere. I was at recovery conventions and doing workshops, public gatherings, and advocacy events. I was on fire! I was speaking in the schools, for state programs, in the jails and juveniles. You name it, I was definitely in high demand. I began learning that God had used my music career to train me to be comfortable on stage speaking. I slowly started

Chapter 5

seeing my past become my pathway to a productive future.

The grass was definitely greener on this side of the tracks, and I was experiencing the best life ever. I was hanging out with people in recovery doing things that were actually fun. For the first time ever, I was living my life. I was no longer a slave to my thinking. It sucks being your own slave and own slave master at the same time. I no longer had to get up and chase a chemical to change the way I felt. I was going to campouts, spending days at the lake. Concerts and sober parties. I had started dating Chelsea, and we were going to movies and just having fun. I couldn't believe I waited this long to start living. This was my community—we were all in recovery, and we were keeping each other accountable and drug free. Don't get me wrong; it's not always rainbows and sunshine. There's drama in the recovery community. There are differences of opinions, slander, and gossip. Everything that you've got in normal society, you have in recovery. But I lived through twenty-three years of addiction and prison. Nobody is going to make me give up my clean time. The only person who can do that is me, and today I'm not willing to jeopardize it. The longer I stayed clean the better life got. I started finding myself in meetings with productive, prominent people in the community, people that work for the state government, and leaders. It was crazy: here I was on parole with multiple felonies sitting at the table with my parole officer supervisor. It was a wild ride—and I was sober, so I remember every minute of it. I was showing up at our state capital advocating for recovery. I was getting phone calls from the attorney general's office to go do presentations for the attorney general. People wanted my opinion. They would ask about how we could help people reentering society. I was being included in the important conversations. I had a voice. WE HAD A VOICE! People started believing in me. I was building a following. God had a plan.

Chapter 5

Arkansas Governor Asa Hutchinson and Jimmy 2017

Chapter 6

Chelsea

Before I met Chelsea, every previous relationship I was in was drug driven. How well I would get along with my partner depended on how high we were. Technically, I can't even call them relationships. More like relationSHYTs. I was used to saying and hearing things like this: "You don't love me; you gave me too much water and not enough dope," "I do love you. It was an accident that I slept with him; we were high," or "Girl, if I didn't love you, don't you think I would have slept with her more than twice, huh? Tell me that." Dysfunction at its highest.

The sad part is, I think we believed all that stuff.

Chapter 6

We were lonely and broken people. Our idea of relationships and love revolved around physical feelings of pleasure. Drugs changed the way we felt and so did sex and physical touch. If I was with a girl for more than two weeks, I thought I was in love with her. This is the way it is with anyone who uses drugs. The truth is, you can't really love anyone when you are so consumed with yourself because true love is selfless.

There is an old cliché I've often heard people say, "Find someone who accepts you for who you are, someone who doesn't want you to change." **<u>Do not listen to that bull spit</u>**. That is terrible advice, trust me. Get someone who sees who you have the potential to become, someone who sees past your image, your front, and someone who isn't willing to bite their tongue for your ego or pride.

Thank God that I didn't listen to the old cliché, that I didn't listen when everyone told me that if a woman loved me, I wouldn't need to change. Change was the one thing I did need. I had always had women who would do whatever I wanted them to do and say whatever I wanted them to say. They would never have spoken their true mind to me. I was used to this type of passive, self-protecting women. My father had instilled core beliefs in me that I was the person who ran everything, including women. With me having less than a year clean, no life skills, clueless on how to behave in public, and with absolutely no manners, into my life walks Chelsea.

I remember looking at Chelsea with interest. I wasn't attracted to her, not yet. I kept looking at her whenever I could safely steal a glance at her without getting caught. I remember thinking that she had a big head, really thick, wavy/curly hair. At first I thought she was kind of funny looking. LOL! I heard her share, and I remember thinking she had a pretty voice. I got a chance to look at her since she was sharing, and I thought *well, maybe she is cute.* She had a very magnetic personality; I was just drawn to her.

Apparently I had done something she didn't like. I remember checking my Facebook Messenger and seeing a message from her, and the message simply read, "We got beef."

At this early point in my recovery, I thought I could still be kind of "hood and tough." A com-

Chapter 6

mon misconception is that machismo is important in life. Like many people in early recovery, I thought I was the center of everything and the world owed me something. I hadn't been clean long enough to realize I hadn't contributed to humanity. In early recovery we haven't asked ourselves, "What have I done to make the world a better place?" Not yet.

I had previously messaged a friend of Chelsea's and threatened to beat him up for somebody else. In my eyes I was being helpful and doing a favor to my friend— typical, chaotic thinking of a newcomer. I had less than a year clean. In fact I saw Chelsea the first time when I was picking up my nine-month clean key tag. Chelsea didn't like that injustice of me threatening her friend, and she decided to address it.

So, she messaged me, threatened me! Ha ha ha! "We got beef." It was the cutest thing I've ever seen.

Her threat started a conversation, and that was all I needed. She was an anomaly to me. Everything about her puzzled me. She was outspoken and very opinionated. I was not used to that. I was

Jimmy McGill

used to women who did whatever I wanted them to do. Women who behaved, dressed, and acted how I wanted them to. I was used to people kissing my butt. Chelsea was used to confrontation and sharing her opinion. She immediately made one thing crystal clear: she would not be kissing my butt. In fact, if anything, she would be kicking it.

You can imagine my shock when Chelsea started telling me to pull my pants up and fix my hat, that I looked like an idiot. I didn't know what to say or what to do. I remember thinking *dang, that's new*. I was caught somewhere between fearing her and being attracted to her. I didn't know whether to date her or fight her. So I didn't do either. She pretty much took the steering wheel. I'll never forget the first time we went out; we went to the Waffle House. And like I said, my life skills were at a minimum. The waitress approached the table, and I looked up and immediately said, "Coffee, eggs, and hash browns." Chelsea looked at me like I had two heads. She looked me dead in the eyes—it was a firm look, too; I did time with killers who didn't look that serious—and she said, "Umm, NO, excuse you." She then addressed the waitress

Chapter 6

and said, "Hello, how are you? We will have some water, thank you." Chelsea literally taught me how to behave in a restaurant. I was loud everywhere I went. All I knew was force; I had a real prison ego. I would cuss in public and had no filter. Looking back, I have to totally laugh at myself. I was so obnoxious, with no social graces, and then had the nerve to get offended when Chelsea didn't want to introduce me to her family. I had never been with a woman who didn't want everyone to know she was with me; after all, I was J Bo.

Another thing, she had all these questions, and I was not used to being questioned. I would tell her what I wanted to do, and she would want to know why. Who does that? Who asks why? I had no idea that people were supposed to actually think before they acted. I was pretty much a Neanderthal when Chelsea met me. She kept me in a total state of confusion. I had never been with a woman who displayed the ability to think for herself, someone who knew her worth. It was both terrifying and highly alluring.

When I met Chelsea, I had smoked cigarettes for twenty years. She griped about it nonstop. Every time I went outside to smoke, I knew it would be hell to pay when I walked back in the house. It became clear that I would have to choose between Chelsea or cigarettes. She pestered me and annoyed me to the point that I began to pray for God to give me the strength to quit smoking. God moved in force because suddenly, every time I lit a cigarette, I got the hiccups. Oh man, it went on for days. After almost going insane, I finally quit smoking. It's been four years since I have smoked a cigarette. This is the great thing about Chelsea: she just didn't *just accept me for who I was;* she challenged me to be the person that I was intended to be. She was something new and fascinating to me. She was a real woman, and she was also in recovery. I knew one thing for sure; she was not scared of me at all, and still isn't, by the way. She pestered me about my clothes and where I shopped. She told me that the way I dressed was not appropriate for a man of my age who was a father and trying to be a productive citizen in society. This is why today I mostly just wear suits!

When we first met, I didn't have a job and was struggling to get one. I'm sure you can imagine

Chapter 6

that it was hard for someone with a criminal history like mine to find employment. There was a temporary service in Little Rock that would occasionally call me for a temporary job. So I stayed broke. On more than one occasion, Chelsea paid my phone bill or my rent at my chem-free house. I was trying my hardest and she knew that. For obvious reasons, in the beginning of our relationship, Chelsea was a little ashamed of me, and she didn't want to broadcast that we were in a relationship. She told me more than once, "Don't tell people we are together." At the time, even if she didn't know it, I knew that we would be together for the rest of our lives. I'll never forget the one day that I did what she told me. I told somebody that we weren't together. Eweeee, man! I never did that again and never will! She went off like a bottle rocket. I don't believe that I have ever been quite so confused in my life. She wanted what she wanted; she just didn't know what she wanted, and that confused me even more. Here is something that I have learned from her: a woman has the right to not know what she wants. In fact, it's okay to not have the answers. Being in a successful, productive, and healthy relationship has been one of the most puzzling, difficult, and rewarding aspects of my recovery.

Another thing I've learned about Chelsea is that she has extreme perseverance. If you're reading this and you want to know how she was able to change me, simple. She fought with me till she got her way. She never left, and she wasn't scared to tell me what she thought. She wasn't scared to point out where I was screwing up, and after so much repetition, things slowly started to change. All I knew how to do was react to situations. She encouraged me to respond. She would say, "Pause and think." I would think, "That is the stupidest thing I have ever heard. Who does that?" She would interrupt me as I talked and correct my vocabulary. As embarrassing and frustrating as this was, today I'm so grateful that she did this. After a while I became mindful. As a public speaker, I need to use proper pronunciation and grammar. As a leader in my state, I need to be able to carry on an intelligent conversation. She saw what I had the potential to be way before I did.

The first time I met Chelsea's family, I was a

Chapter 6

nervous wreck. I knew I wasn't the type of guy that they would expect to be with her. They were not the type of family I was used to seeing. My family members got drunk, fought, and stabbed each other. When we got together, we did dope together and got arrested. But this, this was a normal, successful, and productive family. I loved them. I mean literally, they became my family. I talk to her mom and father all the time. I enjoy being around them. I enjoy getting their advice. The way they come together for each other is fascinating to me. It's the type of stuff you see in the movies, not *The Next of Kin* type of movie. They are extremely close, and they stick together in an incredibly positive way. I often wonder what my life would have been like had I grown up with such a family. But then I wouldn't have my story if I had, and there is no need to cry over spilled milk. I now have this wonderful family and I am thankful. I would not be where I am today if not for Chelsea, and we would not be where we are today if it were not for her family.

I'll never forget the day that I called Chelsea's mom and told her I wanted to ask Chelsea to

Jimmy McGill

marry me. I wanted to do it with her blessing. At the time I was working with a minister (the only person who would put me to work) who told me that I should ask Diana for her blessing and that if she said no, then I would need to respect that. I did not like that idea at all. I wanted to marry Chelsea whether her mom said it was okay or not. So there I was: 40 years old, on parole with pending charges, waiting to be sentenced, living in a chem-free residence, and with no car and only a part time job. Yeah, I'm every mother's dream for her little girl. I was terrified to call. But even though Diana had every reason in the world to tell me, "Hell no, you can't marry my daughter," she didn't. I was stunned when she said, "Yes." To this day I can't imagine what made her give her blessing, to trust me with her baby's life!

None of us imagined my future landing where it has today. Only God knew his divine plan. I had complete support from Chelsea's family to marry her, although her dad told me that if I was smart, I would run. Sometimes I kick myself in the butt for not listening to him! Her family went with me to pick out her wedding ring. They pretty much

Chapter 6

completely planned our wedding and covered our honeymoon. It was simply amazing. I had never experienced that type of love and support; I knew I had found my home.

People often say that we are a powerful couple. I know that God paired us perfectly. We both work in recovery; she and I are both peer recovery specialists. We founded Next Step Women, which became Next Step Recovery Housing. She stands beside me, not behind me. We spend most of our time trying to help people, although we do make time for ourselves. We enjoy one another's company; we laugh together, cry together, and, yes, fight together. We have common goals yet are still free to be different. I love her friends and she loves mine. We are a team.

In all of our differences, one thing we have in common is our commitment to our recovery. We talk recovery all the time. Yet I stay out of hers and she stays out of mine. I value her mind. She has a unique quality of being able to tell people the hardcore truth without offending them. I, on the other hand, always get mad when she says something I don't want to hear. I guess it's the guy in me.

Jimmy McGill

McGill Wedding

Part of my amends process is to treat her like a queen. There were many women that I mistreated, and I will make that right by a living amends of being the best husband that I can be. Most of our arguments today are about if I'm eating healthfully or not. I never thought I'd have to fight over my dinner. So, fellas, if you want to remain the decision maker in what you eat, just don't get married!

Chelsea and I are both active in a 12-step fellowship. We must have a very good balance pertaining to the kids. When we go to our recovery meetings, we don't take the kids if we can help it. She will go to her meetings, and I will keep the

Chapter 6

kids. I have a couple of set days during the week that are my meeting days, and she'll keep the kids. The reasons we don't like to take our children to meetings is that there are a lot of people outside smoking cigarettes and cussing, talking about adult issues, and also there are things shared in a meeting that a child doesn't need to hear. They have heard enough of the war stories when we were high, and frankly they experienced it first hand. Now that we're clean and living life in recovery, they don't need to experience it all over again.

Some of the areas that I struggle in are communication skills and sharing the decision making. A lot of my life was spent using and abusing chemicals. I neglected most chances that I had. I didn't have time to learn how to be a man. I didn't have good role models. Don't get me wrong, my dad was my best friend. I loved him more than anything in the world. But I'm definitely not the kind of dad to my son that my dad was to me. We never did anything fun together. So every day I look at Chelsea and my kids, and I make sure to live my life on purpose and enjoy them and allow them to enjoy me.

Jimmy McGill

All in all, getting married was one of the best decisions I've made in my recovery. God placed the right woman in my life at the right time. More than once I've looked up at the sky and said to God, "You knew that she was hard headed when you gave her to me." I wouldn't trade her for anything.

Jimmy and Chelsea

Chapter 6

McGill Family

Jimmy McGill

McGill Wedding

Chapter 6

Chapter 7

Cindy

For a long time, I struggled with my feelings surrounding my mother. I was ambivalent to say the least. I knew I had siblings that had a better life than I had, and I often wondered what my life would be like had I received the same chances. My dad definitely made it hard for any woman to be with him, and from what I understand he made it next to impossible for Cindy. I remember hearing stories of how bad it was for her. I know that he laid bullets out and told her where each bullet would go into her body. I know she had to jump out of a moving car while she was pregnant with me *(probably banged my head—lol, that would explain a*

Chapter 7

lot).

After a few years of ongoing torture and abuse in every fashion, my mom finally mustered up the courage to run away from my dad. Unfortunately, when the chance finally presented itself, I was not with her. I was only six months old. She had convinced herself that if she ran, she would have the opportunity to come back for me. But that's not the way it worked out. My dad had other plans; he was in love with Linda. At least it was his version of love. So he gave me to Linda, and it would be fourteen years before I would meet my biological mother.

At eleven years old, I learned I had a half-brother named Bobby Strickland. My dad and everyone else knew of Bobby. But I was the last to know. I was living with Linda in Georgia when Bobby reached out to me. He had gotten my number from my father and called me. I was excited and wanted to hear all about his life. We had several long conversations and were excited about the chance of getting to know each other. He was extremely popular in Little Rock, and I wanted to be a part of that; however, I was stuck in Savannah,

Jimmy McGill

Georgia. Bobby and I never actually got to meet because before that could happen, he died in an auto accident. It was at his funeral that I met my birth mother. Bobby had been involved in a police chase. He was riding in a stolen vehicle with two other people. The two other people survived the crash. Bobby, however, did not. He flew out of the windshield and hit his head on a tree. Sadly, tragedy has a way of bringing everybody together.

Shortly after meeting my mother, I decided to go to Pensacola, Florida on spring break. My father let me go. After seeing the life that my younger brothers Chris, Cody, and Camren had with my mother, I was envious and excited. I wanted a piece of that life. They were like the kids I always saw who had it all. They had stability and a safe and secure home life. It was kind of perfect. Not too strict, either. Cindy and my stepdad Joe were willing to allow me the chance; however, my behavior was not conducive to their environment. Within a matter of four weeks, I had them both convinced that I was the devil incarnate. I had been in trouble at school and home. I had bought a silver cap gun from the local drug store and was carrying it

Chapter 7

around like it was a real gun. During a brotherly argument with younger brother Chris one morning, I threw it at him. I missed Chris, but I didn't miss the wall and knocked a softball-sized hole in my mom's wall. At that time Chris and I didn't get along well. A week later I snuck out with a neighbor kid. We stole his dad's truck, and one of us had the bright idea that I should drive. Why? I have no idea. I had never driven before in my life, and of course we wrecked. After that I came back to my Dad in Arkansas. It would be decades before Cindy and I reconnected.

Recovery brought changes to all areas of my life. It completely changed my way of thinking. Among many other things, my recovery brought restoration in my relationship with my biological mother. A few years into my recovery, Cindy found me through social media. There are a few things in life that once they are gone, they're gone. No do-overs. The loss of a parent is one of those. When my stepmother Linda died, I mourned her and I let go. I knew my mom was gone. Then once I found recovery and was able to sustain it, God did the impossible for me again. He gave me an-

Jimmy McGill

other chance at being a son. He also gave Cindy a chance at being my mother. Today we have a great relationship. We chat quite a bit, and we see each other a couple of times a year. I am forming a decent relationship with my brother Cody; he is pretty awesome. And Joe, my stepdad, knows the way to my heart. He feeds me steak every time he sees me. We are all healing now. Nothing is impossible with God.

Chapter 7

Jimmy with Cindy

Chapter 8

God

Ray Charles, blind as he was, could see that God loves me. For me to deny it would be a flat out lie! My story equals God's glory. I am imperfect in every way. I am as screwed up as one can get. Regardless of what I have done, I have a God who took the broken pieces of my life and restructured me into a masterpiece, an instrument of His will. I would not be where I am today if it were not for my relationship with God. He gave me the platform that I have today. His mercy is why I get to help so many people who struggle with addiction. Everything about my life is full of impossibilities that only One far greater than myself could have

Chapter 8

orchestrated and coordinated.

Thank God for mercy and grace within justice. If I had received what I actually deserved, then I wouldn't be typing right now. I would be stripped bare and beaten daily. I would be locked in a cage underneath a prison somewhere living off of two pieces of bread and one cup of water a week. One thing I've learned is that God does not waste any opportunity to show the world His glory. As grateful as I am for the gift of recovery, it is important that I don't forget the Giver of the gift. Which is better, to glorify the gift or the Giver?

Before I began my path of recovery, my relationship with God was one-sided. My prayers were very selfish. It was usual for me to pray in a time of need or when the police were close. I can't count the times I got too high and scared myself, then immediately began praying to God to forgive me because I thought I was dying, and then the empty promises would begin. "God, if You will just let me survive this, I will not get high again." I would pray that the Lord would not let the policeman pull me over and find my bag of dope. "God, if you let me get through this without going to jail, I swear I will straighten up." I would be sitting in a courtroom and praying for the judge to have leniency on me instead of praying for God's will. I would pray selfishly for what I specifically wanted, like the prayers that I would find a cosigner for my bond so someone could bail me out of jail.

Today I am a Christian, and I do believe in Jesus Christ. Today my prayers are different. I pray for others, and I pray for God's will in my life and the strength to be obedient and carry out his will. It is not all about me. I am not a perfect person, and as with most people, I have times that I struggle with my faith. I sometimes wonder if I believe in Christ because I've been taught that all my life or because it's actual truth. Every day for over five years, I've gotten up and read my Bible and prayed. I find great comfort in knowing that the disciples themselves struggled with believing, and they were in the presence of Jesus, walking with him, talking with him, and living with him. Knowing that they went on to carry the gospel to the entire world for generations after the crucifixion definitely makes it more bearable for me when I struggle. I mean, let's be real, the Bible is not an easy concept to buy

Chapter 8

into. A God that took human form was born from a virgin, then later in life crucified and resurrected. But, is it really that hard to believe if you believe that God created the world and the universe, the stars, the sky, the ocean? As difficult as faith is, who am I to question God? I can't just pick and choose which parts of the scriptures I want to believe. I've gotten up and chased after God for years. I plan to continue. My church attendance is not always at its best, but I am a member of That.Church in Sherwood, Arkansas. I pay my tithes, and I have found Malachi 3:10 to be the truth. God has blessed me beyond measure. My personal experience with the Bible is that God is faithful to His Word. I teach my children about God; we do Bible studies, and we pray together. I will continue to chase God. I know every prayer will strengthen my faith in Jesus more and more.

Currently my faith is increasing daily. I have gotten with leadership at my church, and with their blessings I have started a Monday night recovery meeting. It has been extremely successful. It seems to be part of our church now. It's similar to the twelve-step meeting; however, we keep Christ at the center of our recovery. It's not a replacement group; in fact, we encourage attendance at other meetings as well. This is a meeting where we can keep Jesus in the front of our recovery, grow spiritually, and learn how to have a relationship with God. We have built our identity as people in recovery and are welcome at That.Church. We started with ten people meeting at the pizza parlor. We outgrew that location, and the church let us use the church house at the end of the parking lot—we outgrew that one too! Now we're in the student ministry building, and we are about to outgrow that. It's amazing to watch God do what he does and how he uses people who are considered broken vessels to do amazing things. I'm truly humbled and honored to be a part of this journey. I'm in the passenger seat latched in and God is driving. When a person stays clean and gives God the glory, the sky is truly the limit, and there's no telling what He plans to do with each one of us. We have no idea of the life He has in store for us.

Chapter 8

Chapter 9

J Dub

I hit my bottom (breaking point with drug use) while serving time in Lonoke County jail with my cellmate whose name was J Dub. I will never forget the discouragement I felt on that last day I used. I've been taught that if I ever forget the pain and misery on that final day of using, then I haven't had my final day of using. That moment of pain becomes a brief moment of desperation. Desperation is a gift. For people trapped in the grip of addiction, it is only by one sheer moment of desperation that we seek out a new way to live.

J Dub's real name was John Wilson. We met while serving time at the Wrightsville Unit, one of

Chapter 9

Arkansas's many penitentiaries. Wrightsville was once a youth reform school that later became a prison. It was set up like a college campus of sorts, basically dormitories inside of a double-layered barbed wire and razor wire fence, so if you made it through one fence, five feet further was another fence. Wrightsville was what people called a gravy unit, meaning that it was a cakewalk. It was the prison that all inmates wanted to be sent to. Because of the dormitory style housing, there was a lot of traffic and movement going on. Any incarceration that includes inmates moving nonstop is a solid indicator that there is a lot of high-demand contraband, a lot of hustling, and every convict is trying to hustle up some commissary. Since everything was located away from the barracks, you had to go outside to go to work, chow call, yard call, church, visitation, the gym, everything.

I don't remember why I was doing time or what year it was. I'm sure whatever my charge was it had to do with theft. That was my go-to when it came to getting my drugs, and drugs were my motivation for living. I can't remember for sure, but John was probably there on a drug charge. Cigarettes were cheap at Wrightsville—$10 for a pack up top, a dollar (box of cakes) for one roll up. We were living good to be locked up. We were hitting for green money on the visitation yard. We were having packs of tobacco dropped off on the prison property, and the tractor drivers or other outside trustees would get them and sneak them in for a percentage. There were even times that we had piles of methamphetamines. We would buy syringes from the medical trustee that worked in the infirmary at $5 a pop. It sucked being high in prison, but I did it anyway.

John and I hung out a lot, and we were on the same job. We were always cracking jokes and laughing at everything. We were always shooting dice with other inmates, gambling on football games, and hustling up cigarettes. As I said before, the cigarette business is a goldmine in prison. I often joke when I speak that if you are in recovery and think that Roman (ramen) noodles and cigarettes are currency, you're in the right place.

We clicked instantly; he was a standup guy. He was funny, charismatic, and laid back. After we were both released from prison, John and

Chapter 9

I hooked up. He was hard to handle, and when he was drinking, he was the polar opposite of the guy with whom I did time. When he was drunk, he was combative and argumentative. If he had been drinking, he was simply hard to be around. It wasn't John—it was alcoholism. Alcohol tends to have that effect on many people, including myself. It didn't take long to realize John and I didn't need to drink around each other. We were better off just doing dope; at least we could hustle decently together.

John was with me in Lonoke County jail when I hit my bottom. We had been made trustees by the sheriff and moved up front. John and I shared a cell together. Once again, we had made doing time a cakewalk, and we had it good in there. We had a big screen TV, coffee pot, and a DVD player in our cell. We were living the good life considering our location, and out of nowhere I came face to face with my demons. Some dope had made it way inside the jail and right into John's hands. He was like a starving dog on a bone when that dope hit the jail. It was the only thing he was thinking and talking about. I, on the other hand, had absolutely no desire whatsoever to put one (do dope) in me. Moreover, the thought of using made me sick to my stomach. There I was, sitting in jail, on my way back to prison, my life ruined, and I had accepted the fact that I wouldn't be released from the joint until I was too old to enjoy life. All because of my drug use. My mind was made up, and with a one-hundred percent conviction, I looked John in his eyes and told him I was not going to get high. He laughed and said, "Yes, you are." I sarcastically laughed back at him in a mocking way and said, "No, I'm not." Hours continued to pass as John persistently pestered me to use with him. I must have said no fifteen times that day. But it wasn't enough! I said no until I couldn't say no. Sadly, I used with John, and I instantly hated myself for it. I felt terrible.

As we talked about earlier in my book, my decision-making skills are minimal when I'm high. John and I had enough dope to share with several of the units inside the jail. Now, I don't know if you've ever done time; if you have, you'll understand this. If not allow me to educate you. When you're locked up, you eat absolutely everything on

Chapter 9

your food tray. EVERYTHING. You won't leave so much as a ketchup stain. Most jails/prisons feed you the bare minimum, whatever the requirements are by the Department of Health on nutrition guidelines. Most people incarcerated have been starving and neglecting themselves of well-balanced meals due to drug use. We try to make up for our lack of eating starting the second we hit book-in (the jail intake process). You seldom see a food tray without an empty slot on it. Here's how it happened.

John and I shared the dope we had with almost all of the housing units in that jail. Probably for the first time in the history of existence of American jails, every housing unit sent their food trays out untouched. Well, that is, except for John and me. We're smart dope fiends—we decided to scrape our food off in the toilet so it would look like we ate. We were going to fool the sheriff. With us being the only two inmates in the entire jail that ate their lunch, we were the first two that the sheriff drug tested. LOL!

That was February 17, 2015. We spent a week in the hole, and three days later I was in prison. I

Jimmy McGill

chose my clean date because it was the day I hit prison, and I knew the dope was out of my system. February 27, 2015 was the day my life truly began.

The last person I used with was John; we used in Lonoke County Jail, and I have been clean since. John never stopped. I received a sad call from the sheriff on November 5, 2020. Sheriff Staley told me that John was found dead that day. The drug didn't kill him; the lifestyle did!

I tried to plant hope in John once or twice along my journey. He met me at a meeting once and laughed at me. He said, "Bro, you really think those folks are clean?" I said, "Most are." He laughed and said, "Bro, you are tripping." He hugged me. We said, "I love you," and I had no idea that would be the last time I would see my friend. He was a good guy when he was clean.

The disease promises three ends: incarceration, insanity, and death. We either get clean or meet our end.

Chapter 9

John and I at Lonoke County Jail February 2015

Chapter 10

Relationships

Before recovery I had no healthy relationships. Anyone who loved me or even liked me would quickly change their mind when they encountered the real me in my obsession to use. Their affection would turn to disgust. Not only did I run from them, but I burned those bridges. People in addiction don't know how to have relationships. All we know how to do is to take advantage of people who want to help us so that we can manage our obsession with drugs. By "manage the obsession", I'm saying I know how to find a way to get high. The only thing that really ever mattered to me was getting what I wanted, getting my way. Honestly, that

Chapter 10

behavior didn't really stop when I found my recovery. Still today with five years in recovery, I get very aggravated when I don't get my way, especially if I'm dealing with my wife. If I don't get what I want from people, then I'm aggravated and gloomy, which makes absolutely no sense unless you look at it being from the core of my self-centeredness.

Recovery has taught me to look at the disease of addiction logically. I don't want to do what everybody expects me to do, so why do I get mad when they don't want to do what I want them to do? What the heck did I know about relationships? My idea of a solid, healthy relationship was when I was able to pay the dope man for the front he gave me. I called that a working relationship.

A healthy relationship requires the ability for both parties to be able to communicate with each other, to trust one another, and to be open minded to each other's point of view instead of one's own. One has to be willing to contribute his or her part to make the relationship work successfully. No one in active addiction knows how to do any of that.

Presently I have a lot of different types of relationships: mentorship, sponsorship, professional,

Jimmy McGill

my relationship with God, my children, friendship, and so on, none of which I was successful at when I was high. Recovery has opened the door to so many new and fulfilling relationships. My professional relationships are probably some of the most responsible for my personal growth and maturity.

The only professional people I ever knew before were lawyers, prosecutors, correctional officers, and police officers. Sadly, they were some of the most consistent relationships in my life. That was the extent of my experience with professional relationships. I never really had a job, so I never really knew how to work under a supervisor. Not only did I not know how to work, but I would get offended if someone told me to do something that I didn't know how to do. Once I found sustainable recovery, learning how to have professional relationships was a whole new fight all by itself. I had to learn to work collaboratively with my coworkers. Shared decision-making was something I not only did not know how to do but also something I wasn't very willing to do. After all, why in the world would I want to share a decision; what could someone else know that I didn't already know? Sometimes think-

Chapter 10

ing back brings me a ping of embarrassment. How could I have been so full of myself and unteachable? I mean, me with my eighth-grade education and my six prison stints must surely be superior to everyone else. At least I can laugh at myself. Let's just say, I've come a long way. I'm not afraid to say, "I don't know," and I really appreciate the gifted professionals in my life and have become one myself.

Prior to finding sustained recovery, a true friendship was completely foreign to me. The closest thing I knew to friendship was that occasionally I'll get you high and when I'm out you get me high. This would make us the best of buddies. Where I came from, your friends break into your house and steal your stuff as soon as you go to jail, because it's a safe time to get away with it. Friendship was reptilian; everybody was a snake. Everyone in my world double crossed one another. Everybody loudly promised that they wouldn't tell anything, that they would keep their mouth shut and take a secret to the grave even if they got caught committing a crime. Then as soon as they got to the central book-in, they wrote a statement on you. They

Jimmy McGill

got released, and you sat in the holding cell jonesing (desiring to get high).

Today my relationships are real. I am not just a taker. I am a giver and do my part to make my relationships successful. It took a couple of years before I was able to listen to other people. But because of many patient people, I've learned and grown. This brings to mind my sponsor, who is really good at telling me things I do not really want to hear. But I'm thankful for the sandpaper.

Chapter 10

Chapter 11

Next Step

I can't think of anything that has led to more arguments with my wife than Next Step Recovery Housing. Next Step is a 501(c)(3) nonprofit organization that my wife and I founded. There are very few things in early recovery as important as a sober living home, a place where addicts and alcoholics in the early processes of addiction recovery can have a safe and stable living environment. While using and abusing, we neglected the simple, everyday life skills that most people learned at an early age. Our life skills consisted of chasing and finding more alcohol and drugs.

While living the addiction lifestyle, we really

Chapter 11

don't know how to live everyday life. Problem solving is out of the question. Our idea of cooking a good dinner is microwaving a ramen noodle packet or opening a snack cake and a Coke.

This is why a recovery home is so important. These homes are called any number of things: sober living homes, chemical free houses, chem-free, or recovery residences. The names may change, but the mission is the same.

Since I found my recovery through a chem-free house, I know the importance of one better than do most people. Recovery housing is one of my biggest passions. I believe gratitude is an action word, and for me, being as grateful as I am for the gift of recovery, I need to show that gratitude by putting it into action and being the change that I want to see.

From the time that I met my wife, we have overseen sober living houses, whether it was our own or someone else's. To say that Chelsea and I were successful at running a recovery residence would be a major understatement. Most people would consider our foundation to be the model recovery residence in the state. We built Next Step from guidelines and best practices of the National Alliance of Recovery Residences (NARR).

We learned a lot over the years. We've had bad experiences with bad partners and good experiences with good partners. We have had ups and downs of every variation. Honestly, there is no way to put into words the blood, sweat, and tears that my wife and I have put into this foundation. There've been endless nights, fights, laughs, unyielding tears, joy, and pain; and it has all been for the sake of other people—a desire to help others because we were helped.

One of the hardest things about running a recovery program is how ungrateful those you are trying to help can be. Regardless of how much we would do for people, they never seemed to appreciate it. Honestly, addicts can be very similar in their attitudes and thinking to children. We sometimes refer to them as adult children. There are a lot of pressures when one steps out to run recovery programs. Not only do you get to deal with all of the arguing, fighting, and disrespect from the very people you're trying to help, but you also have others in the recovery community critiquing all of

Chapter 11

your decisions. Everyone has an opinion that they are more than willing to share. Some have a true desire to help; but others because of jealousy, bitterness, and other things are simply judging you while sitting on their butts doing nothing. One thing for sure, walking through the fire of reaching out to people in addiction will refine true motives. You will know you're in for the right reasons when you power up and push through all of the negative emotions, when you show up regardless of your feelings and the feelings of others and press on with your head high knowing that you're doing this for no other reason than compassion. If anyone reading this is even slightly thinking of opening sober living homes to make money, give up now. I mean, literally, abandon that idea quickly! In actuality, it will cost you a ton of personal time, effort, and money. Most people truly making a difference pay to help, not the other way around. The only thing you get when you provide service to people out of passion is happiness mixed with heartache.

I stayed in a sober living facility for about thirteen months. For the first few years of my recovery, my wife and I helped our friend Terrell develop

Jimmy McGill

his recovery residences. When Terrell hired me, he had two Arkansas Community Corrections (ACC) licensed transitional houses. I developed policies, procedures, rules, and regulations. I was good at it because of my lived experience with sober living homes. We expanded, and within the first year we had three more houses up and running, two additional men's homes and one female home. Chelsea was over the women's house. We tweaked the rules and regulations that I had developed for the men's houses just enough to be an appropriate fit for the female home, and we applied them. Terrell is a good businessman, a true visionary. He could see a project in raw form and visualize what it could be. With his vision and business mindset and my knowledge of recovery and reentry, we quickly grew Freshly Renewed to be the largest sober living organization in Pulaski County, Arkansas.

Eventually my wife and I opened our own recovery home. I think all people in recovery have the potential to do amazing things. Anyone with the ability to start every morning with nothing and finish the day off with exactly what is needed has a powerful skill. When we learn to apply that in

Chapter 11

an acceptable, productive, and positive manner, we can achieve anything. Truthfully, addicts are very ingenious people. They are incredibly skilled at accomplishing the impossible. One could literally put a person in active addiction on one side of the Grand Canyon with a pipe and dope, and then another person in addiction on the opposite side with a lighter, and they would find a way to smoke. Ingenuity at its finest—but not with a worthy goal. So, when you take an addict and add recovery and faith, there you will find a powerful individual to work positive change in a challenging environment.

Next Step began as a women's home. Chelsea felt called to open a home, and a friend of ours provided a location in a house in Cabot, Arkansas. Chelsea literally quit her job at the Bridgeway Hospital where she was employed as a Mental Health Professional to chase after what she felt like she was being called to do. I was worried because I knew we didn't have any money for operations and that we would have to carry the burden of watching our dream grow. Thank God for His people, though! Chelsea got a part time job as she ran the house. Our friends Gage and Amber, who own

Jimmy McGill

Amber's Goochie Poochie (a dog grooming shop in North Little Rock), gave Chelsea a job and worked with her on a schedule that was convenient. It allowed her to focus on the House and offered a financial solution. God was providing for us. Honestly, I think that's what got Chelsea through the first year of chaos as we were learning ups and downs of the recovery house. If it weren't for being surrounded by positive, godly people like Amber and Stephanie, we probably would have killed each other that first year. Chelsea was rooted in a positive atmosphere where she could get God's word poured into her. When the stress became overwhelming, the women would pray.

In Next Step's Cabot location, we filled up quickly. We thought because we had a lot of bodies in the house that our program was successful. This could not have been further from the truth. It takes way more than just numbers to sustain a program. Finances were a constant concern, and business disagreements with the person who had put up the house for us caused a lot of problems. We quickly learned that it was prayer time. People minimize the power of prayer; however, in reality it is the

Chapter 11

strongest weapon that we as human beings have. We can go to the creator of all the second we need him. We can lay our case at his feet. One thing about my life that God has made evident is that I belong to him. Everything around me belongs to him, and he will shape and reshape my future as he sees fit. So despite the odds or how negative the situation may appear to be, God does the impossible all the time, and he uses ordinary people to do extraordinary things. I'm proof of this, and my wife is proof of this; Next Step is proof of this!

It didn't take long, a couple of weeks of consistent prayer, and then God moved in force. We were praying for a house big enough to house the women that we envisioned. We needed a house cheap enough that the women working and contributing $100 a week would allow it to sustain itself. God did that! He gave us a house that was almost twice the size and half the rent. The first four months were rent free! That four months gave us the chance to save up funding and raise money. God was showing up and showing out.

My church has a men's ministry called Point Man, and all of Point Man showed up and helped us move. We had done the impossible in a matter of two days, moved and remodeled like it was nothing. We had media attention coming from everywhere, and people were donating left and right. God was making a way. Next Step had moved to Sherwood, Arkansas, three miles from where my wife and I lived. It made building that nonprofit into a successful organization a lot easier.

The most beautiful thing about the Sherwood house is that it was my aunt Juanita's house, the house where I met God, the house where I was prayed over, where one godly woman would raise dozens of godly people and pray over hundreds. My aunt Juanita was looking down from heaven at the boy she spent more time praying over than anyone else and seeing me do God's work.

Right beside the Sherwood house was my grandfather's old house. This was the place where my addiction had started. My first memories of holding off my father's arms so he could find a vein to shoot cocaine were in that house. And here I was right back where I started on a brand-new mission. Like so many things in my life, God had brought me full circle, from pain and despera-

Chapter 11

tion to passion and hope. Addicts' lives may have started there, but powerful, renewed lives now resided there.

We saw a lot of successful women emerge sober out of the Next Step Women's House. I often think of Sierra and Taylor, both young and beautiful with their whole lives in front of them. Back then they were an enormous pain in my butt. They argued with me, forgot to do their chores, and had attitudes including a little bit of entitlement. But wow, the change has been amazing!

Honestly, they're like our children at this point. I can't imagine our lives without Taylor and Sierra. The random text messages that they send on progress and struggles are the highlights of my day. They don't call or text as much these days, but we are here when they need us. They are living life to the fullest.

Taylor and Sierra are not the only success stories to emerge from Next Step. Another warming story is Caitlin. She struggled for a long time in and out of recovery. She could never get more than a few months clean. Chelsea always saw something in Caitlin. It took me a little longer to see it. Chelsea was right—Caitlin was a fighter and a survivor. Despite the things that were stacked against her or the people who doubted her, today she is over a year clean and sober, and she has become a mother of which her daughter can be proud. We've had women who have received their nursing licenses and peer recovery certifications and have gone to work for treatment centers.

I could spend days writing about the successes of which God has let my wife and me be a part. It's times like when we watch women graduate or get a job that they never thought they could get that makes the hard work all worth it.

That's where our reward is; that's why we do what we do—to watch people who society thinks are hopeless become beacons of hope. They survive the flames and become a light in the darkness.

People in recovery from drug addiction are true examples of a phoenix that rises out of the ashes.

We had been in Sherwood for about six months when That.Church Pastor Scott wanted to meet with me. The church partnered with us. I couldn't believe it. They agreed to make monthly donations! Next Step did not have to worry nearly as

Chapter 11

much as it had before. The That.Church family believed in what Chelsea and I were doing. This was not only helpful on the financial side, but also to know that people believed in us and what we were doing and wanted to be a part of the solution for our community. It was a game changer.

As we continued to grow and help people, we began to pray for God to guide us and expand us. We had now been in Sherwood for eighteen months. We thought we were stable until suddenly our landlord sold the house out from under us. We made a solid offer on the house, but in a world where money rules over ministry, we lost out. When this happed it seemed like a catastrophe to us, but where there are catastrophic situations, God has a chance to showcase His power and glory.

A week before this sale occurred, an unexpected miracle happened. Her name is Sharon Garrett. We didn't know it, but God was sending a life raft from Clarksville, Arkansas.

Sharon Garrett and her family had previously been the financial backing behind a ministry called Proving Grounds, which reached out to men in recovery through a program and a sober living

Jimmy McGill

house. Due to unforeseen circumstances, Proving Grounds was closing down, and they and their church were trying to figure out what to do with the house and the ministry. It is crystal clear to me that God connected us. Both the Clarksville mission to men in recovery and Next Step would have been dissolved by now if it weren't for the partnership that God put together at that time.

It was one day during the COVID-19 lockdowns when I was working from my home that my phone rang. The very fact that I would answer an unknown number during a time when my phone was constantly blowing up is a miracle in itself. But as God would have it, I took the call and Sharon was on the other end of the line. She lined out the dilemma they were currently in and asked if I knew anyone who would be interested in stepping in and saving this ministry. Sharon had heard me speak at a meeting the previous fall and knew me to be passionate about recovery. I was stunned at the call. My pastor and I got together to take a drive up to Clarksville. We enjoyed the drive. On a side note, I enjoy any time I get to be one-on-one with Scott Harness. I often find myself depleted from pour-

Chapter 11

ing into others, so mentorship between me and my spiritual advisor is a welcome relief. It's a time that I can I get my cup refilled. Back to the story, Scott and I spent several hours with them discussing addiction, recovery, ministry, and Jesus. I learned a few things about Scott that day. First and foremost is that my pastor is saved but not soft! He is freaking hardcore when it comes to business, shrewd and sharp. He guided me through that process. Our biggest concern was the logistics of running a home an hour and a half from Little Rock, where I was located. We were concerned about jobs for the men and things like that.

However, the house has remained at capacity from the day we opened it. All men are working and living their best life. They go to church weekly, do Bible studies, and receive peer support services and case management. The distance has not kept us from being able to invest in them the way we want. The program has been an extremely successful program.

Two months into the Clarksville house, God brought me full circle again. The Arkansas Community Correction's (ACC) transitional license is one of the hardest things for a recovery home to receive. To get this license requires that a home/program meet the ACC standards of excellence. A license from the state of Arkansas's probation and parole services says that you meet all the state standards and requirements to be allowed to house multiple people on probation and parole in the same house. We did this and are so proud to have this licensure.

Most people in addiction also have very colorful criminal histories. Our biggest sin is worse than singing too loudly in church. It's incredibly hard to overcome addiction and all of the legal issues we have. So to be a facility that's allowed to house and offer services to people on parole is simply phenomenal! I was once a parolee at an ACC house, and now God has allowed me to partner with the ACC so that I can house men who are on parole. That license was a landmark achievement for Next Step.

The same month we received our license, we received a second huge blessing. One of our board members, Paula Cunningham, a beautiful soul who lost her son to addiction and founded her own non-

Chapter 11

profit, the Parker Gill Foundation, raised a $50,000 donation for Next Step.

Because of this incredible donation, we were able to expand from six beds to eight and buy our housing manager an RV camper. We have continued to be able to manage the property and the program.

Next Step has continued to set the bar for recovery residences in Arkansas. We are so thankful for those who have partnered with us to do this great work. We are so grateful for That.Church, Parker Gill Foundation, Safe Haven Ministries, Inc. (a women's ministry in Clarksville), and many people who have donated and continue to donate to Next Step. We endeavor to be an organization that invests in people both physically and spiritually. We want to save people's souls and redeem their lives. We do not believe people are the sum total of their addiction; rather, we believe they are the sum total of the value God Himself has placed on them.

Next Step wouldn't be where we are today without our Board of Directors. So, allow me to say a huge thank you to Macy Wadley (Board President), Paula Cunningham (Vice President), Bruce Garrett

Jimmy McGill

(Treasurer), and Stacy Harness (Secretary).

I would also like to say thank you to two incredibly special people that are dear to my heart and our organization: to Joseph Cruz, our housing manager, for being an inspiration and an example to the men on a daily basis and also to Brett Franks, one of my closest friends, who has been beside me from the beginning. Brett is probably the most selfless person that I know, and although he is not a part of our staff, our dream is to grow to the point that he will be. Brett volunteers on a regular basis. He drives up one weekend a month to give Joseph some time off. He's always at our events and goes above and beyond to be of service to the community.

Anyone who would like to donate to our 501(c)(3) nonprofit can do so through our website nextsteprecoveryhousing.org.

Currently we're in constant prayer that God will give us the resources to be able to put a Next Step home in all seventy-five counties in Arkansas. We want to be the premier recovery residence program in the state. We believe this is possible with the help of God and compassionate people who want to help (hint, hint—that's you).

Chapter 11

In closing, I want to say that I think the greatest thing that has come out of our move to Clarksville is my relationship with Bruce and Sharon Garrett.

Sharon and I are a lot alike. We are on a remarkably similar mission. She reminds me of my Aunt Juanita. She's a little bit feistier, a small pack of dynamite if you get her hyped up! I often wonder if she has a little dose of a drug addict inside. Sharon and I have a lot of conversations around mission work. Her authenticity as a Christian inspires me. She lets me know that I can be myself (imperfect in every way), and God still loves me. Oh, and I can't forget, she is one of the people editing this book, so—BIG THANKS to you, Sharon.

Jimmy McGill

Jimmy and Chelsea with Taylor

Jimmy and Chelsea with Joseph

Chapter 11

Chapter 12

The Recovery Clinic

COVID-19 brought many changes, one of them being The Recovery Clinic, an innovative idea of using social media to maintain recovery support and services. As the pandemic lockdowns progressed in the state of Arkansas, so did relapse rates. People were returning to drug use at an astronomical rate. Naloxone administration rates tripled, which insinuated that the overdose rates were actually higher since we only track the naloxone saves. Suicide rates spiked as well. Suddenly the recovery community was shutting down. CrossFit, 12-step meetings, gyms, yoga, churches, and self-help groups were all closing. Everything that

Chapter 12

had helped us maintain our personal recovery was abruptly stripped away. But one thing stayed with us… ADDICTION. The obsession to use was lurking around in the minds of addicts everywhere. People in long-term

recovery, who had been pillars in the recovery community, were suddenly drinking and using again. COVID-19 didn't close the dope houses; addiction was in full force. People were dying. I decided to do something about this—The Recovery Clinic.

Being bored and trapped in isolation, I decided to go live from my Facebook page, Jimmy McGill Live. I only wanted to encourage others to not use, but I had no idea it would become a state initiative. Shortly after, I partnered with another guy in recovery to add a new flavor to the show. As polar opposite as we were, we shared a lot of common similarities. We are both dads, husbands, and businessmen; and we are both in long-term recovery. We saw the power of social media, and we saw that it could be harnessed as a tool to reach people everywhere and save lives. We realized we were on to something we couldn't stop. So, we did what we

Jimmy McGill

always do when we find something that's good and impactful. We hit the gas with it.

We started out going live from Facebook two times a week. The message on the recovery clinic was and is "we do recover." We don't have to be an island of one. There is a difference between social isolation and social distancing. The Recovery Clinic offers a way for us to stay connected throughout the pandemic. We don't have to do this alone, even when we have to be alone. We discuss controversial topics, resources, recovery efforts, and more. We bring on guest speakers and interview them and hear their stories. We are essentially a lifeline for people under quarantine. We have regulars awaiting the show, and that's exactly what it is: a social media TV show. That's definitely what it's turned into today.

The state drug czar quickly saw the value in this, and he reached out to me to inquire if I would incorporate this into my job description. That was huge. Shortly after, we found help through unspent funds from our state opioid response (SOR) grant, and before we knew it, we were partnering with the KARK4 and FOX16 news stations. We were

Chapter 12

broadcasting to both our audience and theirs. Production was the highest of quality since we were broadcasting from a news studio. Suddenly we were a relevant, in-demand, and professional television production podcast.

I am still going strong every Wednesday at 11 AM. I have had some amazing guests: Arkansas Governor Asa Hutchinson; John Kirtley, President of the Arkansas Board of Pharmacy; Ryan Hampton; Brian Cuban; and I could go on for days about all the guests we have had. The guest lineup for the next couple of months is pretty exceptional. Maybe you can tune in.

The thing about social media is that it can safely carry a message of hope to people in addiction everywhere. Anyone with a mobile device can randomly hear the message. All it takes is the right person to share the video and the potential is there. They might just hear what they need to hear in order to try something new. I have been taught to keep my personal recovery first! I can't put anything in its way. This means that I can't safely enter the dope house screaming "any addict can stop using". That would put me at great risk; how-

Jimmy McGill

ever, Facebook can go anywhere. So, can TikTok, Twitter, Instagram, and YouTube. Its 2021, social media plays a powerful role in everything including recovery. I thank God that I have bosses that believe in me and understand that I have to stay sober to do my job. Deborah Motley-Bledsoe has been the greatest supervisor I could have asked for. Both she and Kirk have allowed me the daily time to put my recovery first. They fight constantly for these new ideas like "The Recovery Clinic", and they believe in us. I hope you get that type of support in your job!

Chapter 12

Sheriff Staley and I

Chapter 13

Full Circle

My life is definitely coming full circle. If you would have told me five years ago, when I was walking out of prison for my last time, that I would become the first parolee to work for the state of Arkansas, I would have thought you were doing better dope than I had ever done. It's amazing that I spent so much of my life doubting and questioning God, wondering what his plan was for me and why my life was so unfair. I remember sitting in prison with no hope. I had completely given up, didn't even think about freedom. The only thing I lusted for was a woman and a shot of dope. Sitting in a barracks with seventy men, shaking my

Chapter 13

head because the hand that I had been dealt wasn't fair, I had no idea what God had in store for me. There's a Bible verse that often comes to my mind, Jeremiah 29:11, *"For I know the plans I have for you," declares the LORD, "plans to prosper you and not to harm you, plans to give you hope and a future."* His plan is for me to show the entire world what He is able to do for me, and for anyone else living in hopelessness. Everything about my life today goes completely against society's status quo.

I became the first felon to work for the Arkansas Department of Human Services—and not just *any* felon, but one with seventeen felony convictions, while still on parole. Kirk Lane and I had been speaking all over the state of Arkansas, at colleges, high schools, the attorney general's drug summit—you name it, we were sharing a message of hope together. He informed me of a job that would be coming open, and he encouraged me to apply for it. I thought there was absolutely no way in the world that I would receive this job working for the state, especially as the Arkansas Peer Recovery Coordinator. What I didn't know was that a requirement for the job was that you have personal experience with drug addiction and be a person in long-term recovery. I definitely had that part down to a tee! There were four other people who applied for the position. However, they did not have that one requirement needed. They were not recovering addicts. The position also required a degree, which I didn't have. Yet I was currently enrolled in college. The day I interviewed for the job, I was quite intimidated. As I sat in front of a panel of people from the Arkansas Department of Human Services (DHS) with questions flying from all four directions, I was reminded of my last parole hearing. I was prepared, though. I knew recovery. I was an expert on drug addiction. I went into that meeting prepared. I had developed a full launch plan and had printed it out and placed it in folders for each person on the panel. I even impressed myself.

Later, I learned that I blew the doors off of that interview and scored higher than anyone who interviewed. All I could do was hit my knees and praise God and cry. I had hope that I was about to do something that had never before been achieved in the state of Arkansas. There was a lot of blowback, a lot of rumors, and a lot of speculation on

Chapter 13

why the Arkansas Department of Human Services would hire a parolee. It was against state policy. There had never been a felon work for DHS, much less someone actively on parole. Yet I had impressed the supervisors and decision makers with my interview to the point that they advocated for me. When the state said I couldn't, God said I could. When DHS said it's against policy, God said it's My policy.

At the request of Director Kirk Lane, Governor Asa Hutchinson signed off on my background for me to work as a state employee in 2017. In 2019 we even changed state law! Governor Asa Hutchinson signed AR HB1433 into law as Act 951 allowing people with nonviolent criminal histories to work for state agencies as peer support specialists or in similar roles. It was a moment that would change history and shape the future of Arkansas. That day launched us into national leadership for recovery efforts.

For the most part, the support that the State of Arkansas has given me is almost unbelievable. However, when someone who is as publicly outspoken about their past as I am got a job with the

Jimmy McGill

state, it shook things up. I have noticed that people are either supportive of me or they aren't; there is no gray area. I'm sure half of the employees in my division are still waiting for me to steal their car keys, always watching and looking and stigmatizing me. I understand that they are just afraid of what they do not understand.

Today I work for the same boogeyman that I used to hide from. Kirk Lane is no longer the head of the drug task force or the criminal investigation division. He's no longer a police officer. He's the state drug czar, and he believes in recovery because he saw a recovery take place in my life. God knew decades ago when He put that man into my life to arrest me that we would share the podium together, that we would use our story to inspire hope in both people seeking help to recover from addiction and law enforcement officers who need to bear witness that recovery is possible.

From the second I got hired, we changed the game. I knew that I had one chance, and I was not about to waste it. I walked it like I talked it! I knew that I had a lot to prove, but being doubted was nothing new to me. I was used to skepticism. There

Chapter 13

was something inside of me, driving me for success. I knew from the beginning that this was bigger than me, that this was about showing a broken system that a person's past is not a life sentence, that people can overcome anything, and that people in recovery have value and need a seat at the table. Five years ago, my friend Dana B. looked me in the eye and told me, "Jimmy, boy don't f*&% this up; this is about all of us," and her voice still echoes in my mind today. My past became my pathway; my pain transformed into passion. I am an agent of change.

I often look at my life and still cannot believe how far God has carried me. He took my past and turned it into purpose. He took the life that I had made a mess of, and He made that mess into a message, all for His glory. God literally pulled me out of prison and set me on a pathway to a productive future. There were many roadblocks that might have stopped me from having the position and the platform that I have today. So when policy and procedure said, "You've got to have a degree to be a state employee," God said, *"I made the degree."* When policy and procedure said, "Fel-

Jimmy McGill

ons can't work for the state," God said, "*I made the state.*" See, everything in my life before February 27, 2015 was preparation for God to fulfill His amazing purpose in my life. All of my life, all of the suffering, was for the glory of God. God was preparing me for the work that I'm called to do. Even the music era of my life was preparation. As a national leader and advocate for recovery, I often find myself on a stage speaking to a crowd of people, many times a large crowd. I have spoken to groups of people ranging from little country churches with only thirty-five people all the way up to national meetings having two-thousand people. Learning to be comfortable onstage and perform in front of large crowds prepared me for my public platform. It prepared me to be comfortable with a microphone when I step up to share my story. If not for the twenty plus years of addiction, I would not understand recovery or addiction or the process to find and sustain recovery. The six trips to prison were on-the-job training for me. The former gang life—God was preparing me to be able to do something that most people can't do. I'm uniquely qualified to reach and teach a group of people

Chapter 13

most others don't understand and with whom most can't identify. Through a bond of common relation and understanding, I can reach a group of people society has deemed unreachable and unteachable; and if we are going to be honest, people who are perceived as not worth the trouble. I was once the same "write-off." I was the guy considered a failure, the one who was going to die in addiction or spend his life in prison. But I overcame that stigma. I now go back into those same flames that once engulfed me, carrying buckets of water to the ones suffering from addiction. I came out of the fire a refined version of myself.

Today I am the State Opioid Response Coordinator. I have gone on to change history in the State of Arkansas. I'm proud to be a person in long-term recovery; but that is not all I am. I am also a father, husband, a worker, and a supervisor. I'm a homeowner, a member of That.Church in Sherwood, Arkansas, and a contributor to my community, my state, and my nation. My wife and I founded a 501(c)(3) nonprofit recovery foundation for women which has now expanded to working with men. We specialize in housing people and helping them sus-

Jimmy McGill

tain recovery, find employment, and learn everyday life skills. It is called Next Step Recovery Housing. Look us up! Our first home, which was a women's home, was the first home in Arkansas to utilize the peer support approach, which is people in recovery as the key component—completely nonclinical. In the first two years, the house had a total of thirty-two women; twenty-three of those women are in long-term recovery today.

I am positive that when Kirk Lane hired me, he had to have been nervous. If the tables had been turned, I would have been scared to death. He took a huge risk on me when he put all his chips on a person in recovery, and not just any person in recovery but one with a rap sheet ten miles long. I'm sure other state directors and leaders probably thought that he might need a little rehab himself! Yes, we have accomplished great things together and have changed the perception of many people and many agencies. He has become my biggest advocate.

I appreciate the risk he took on me, and I have not let him down. Together we have been able to share a story of cops and robbers with a positive

Chapter 13

ending. We designed and developed peer recovery support in the State of Arkansas. Other states were already doing it, and we were behind the eight ball on it. However, since working together and developing my position, we have jumped in the lead. We have gained national attention for recovery efforts in Arkansas. I'm proud to say that I've had a big part in that.

I am a huge advocate for peer recovery. Peer recovery support specialists are people with direct lived experience from their own addiction. They are people who have survived addiction and now have a minimum of two years of sustained recovery. The state will take them and train them on how to use their recovery to help other people find their recovery. We have also changed history for the State of Arkansas in this area. Within twenty months we have trained 310 peer support specialists. We have also designed the *nation's first* multi-level peer recovery model, and in doing so we created a career ladder. We created the Arkansas model, allowing peers to be supervised by seasoned peers instead of clinicians. Now the peers can become a peer specialist, go on to become an

Jimmy McGill

advanced peer specialist, and then work their way into becoming a peer supervisor. This is workforce development with competitive salaries. We also held the first-ever region six peer recovery conference, pulling all five states in our region together for the purpose of expanding the development of peer recovery. We brought in national speakers and had over 540 people in attendance—it was amazing! Sheriff John Staley, that hard-nosed Lonoke County Sheriff, was also there talking about the peer recovery program that he partnered on with us. The same jail that I got high in for my last time was the first jail to have the peer recovery program that I developed—full circle! This program is currently at a seventy percent success rate, using people with lived experience who have successfully reentered society and today are living clean from addiction. Sheriff Staley and I are close friends now. My favorite times are those rare moments when Kirk, myself, and the sheriff are all three together, hanging out and laughing, telling jokes about my stupidity and how hard-headed I was. I know that I can call on those two men at any time or any place and they will be there for me.

Chapter 13

They have watched me fight through my addiction, through my incarceration, and for my life; and they've stood by me to help me build a new one. I will be forever grateful to them. I know that they were part of God's plan.

It's amazing to walk back into the same jail cell in which I slept and to share a message of hope. When talking with the men in jail, the credibility that I have from spending my life in and out of the same system that they are currently in immediately authenticates the sincerity of recovery. When the fellas see me, they get excited and they yell my name; they come up and hug me; and they are truly happy that one of us has made it out of that life and on to the other side. It's amazing when, a year later, I walk back in that same jail with one of them sharing their recovery. True redemption is what God is giving me.

I am the founding member of the *Arkansas Peers Achieving Recovery Together (*A.P.A.R.T) coalition. I am also the chairman for the Arkansas Peer Advisory Committee (APAC), which is a subcommittee of the Alcohol and Drug Coordinating Council. Because of my situation, Arkansas with HB1433 changed state law by allowing people with nonviolent criminal history to work for state agencies as peer recovery support specialists. Our good governor signed it into law effective January 2, 2020. My wife and I host a yearly anti-stigma kickball tournament between law enforcement and people in recovery. I also designed and developed the *Peers Achieving Collaborative Treatment* (The P.A.C.T) project, allowing the state to place peer recovery in incredibly unique, out-of-the-box positions. We now have recovery specialists in reentry centers, recovery homes, community organizations, the Arkansas Department of Human Service's Division of Youth Services, and jails and drug courts. In all of these places, people are seeing the value of people in recovery. This is my story: a way more than three-time loser becoming a mover and shaker all across this state in an un-trumpeted population of people.

Through God gifting me with the process of recovery and new information and someone to teach me how to apply that information, I have experienced transformation.

Information + application through exemplification = transformation

Chapter 13

Recovery has done so much more than restore me to sanity or give me my life back. It has redefined me; it has restructured a mindset that was corrupted. A lifetime of distorted core values has been changed. I have experienced a true shift in perception. I don't struggle between church and recovery; I know that God is not in competition with the gift that he gave me. Everything about my life has God's fingerprints all over it. I've got to give credit where it's due. If not for God, how else do you explain me walking out of a prison cell and getting clean? It seems like I'm getting onto a plane every other week and flying all over the nation sharing about the possibilities of an alcohol and drug-free life. I'm a repeat offender who has the privilege of sitting at the table with decision makers. I represent an entire community who has been overlooked for decades. I've been able to be a voice for people who don't have a voice. I've overcome obstacles and struggles that most normal people would not have even survived. My trials and tribulations didn't break me; they built me. They made me a creature that God could use for a purpose so much bigger than anything I've ever dreamed of.

Jimmy McGill

The old cliché "broken crayons still color" is revamped by my life testimony that not only do we still color, but we color the brightest. I know, without a shadow of a doubt, that people in recovery have a higher value and appreciation for life than most people. Why? Because when you have lived without something and then finally get it, you appreciate it so much more. We have had to fight for the life we have found. We have climbed and clawed our way out of a self-made hell. Recovery won't necessarily give you the keys to the Kingdom of Heaven—that is between you and God—but it will unlock the gates of your drug-induced, man-made hell and set you free. Recovery has brought my life full circle.

The same officers, who once arrested me, partner with me today. The same jail in which I used to sit and cry and pray, feeling hopeless and helpless, I stand in now as a beacon of hope to inmates who are sitting in the same seats that I once sat in. The same parole officers who once drug tested me and locked me up now reach out to me for help. The same system that I once hated I've had the opportunity to restructure. The same people I blamed for

Chapter 13

all of my problems now get to show me how to be a productive man in society. Where I once was imprisoned, I now have freedom. I went from prison to purpose. Full circle!

Jimmy McGill

Chapter 13

Jimmy McGill

Region 6 Peer Conference 2019

Getting HB1433 signed into law

Chapter 13

Kirk and Jimmy

Advocating for recovery in Arkansas' Supreme Court room

Jimmy McGill

Chapter 13

Made in the USA
Coppell, TX
28 March 2022

75653727R10115